S0-AFN-881

Pocket
LONDON
TOP SIGHTS · LOCAL LIFE · MADE EASY

Emilie Filou

In This Book

QuickStart Guide

Your keys to understanding the city – we help you decide what to do and how to do it

Need to Know
Tips for a smooth trip

Neighbourhoods
What's where

Explore London

The best things to see and do, neighbourhood by neighbourhood

Top Sights
Make the most of your visit

Local Life
The insider's city

The Best of London

The city's highlights in handy lists to help you plan

Best Walks
See the city on foot

London's Best...
The best experiences

Survival Guide

Tips and tricks for a seamless, hassle-free city experience

Getting Around
Travel like a local

Essential Information
Including where to stay

Our selection of the city's best places to eat, drink and experience:

◉ **Sights**

✖ **Eating**

🍷 **Drinking**

✪ **Entertainment**

🔒 **Shopping**

These symbols give you the vital information for each listing:

☏ Telephone Numbers	👪 Family-Friendly
⊘ Opening Hours	🐾 Pet-Friendly
🅿 Parking	🚌 Bus
⊖ Nonsmoking	⛴ Ferry
@ Internet Access	⊖ London Tube
🛜 Wi-Fi Access	🚋 Tram
🥗 Vegetarian Selection	🚆 Train/Overground
📖 English-Language Menu	

Find each listing quickly on maps for each neighbourhood:

Bar Hemingway

16 🍷 Map p233, B2

Legend has it that Hemi self, wielding a machine erate this timber-pan ered bar during en by Papa ar town. Dress com; Hôtel Rit ⊘6.30pm-2a

6 ◉ Plac

Lonely Planet's London

Lonely Planet Pocket Guides are designed to get you straight to the heart of the city.

Inside you'll find all the must-see sights, plus tips to make your visit to each one really memorable. We've split the city into easy-to-navigate s and provided clear maps so you'll find your way around with ease. Our expert authors have searched out the best of the city: walks, food, nightlife and shopping, to name a few. Because you want to explore, our 'Local Life' pages will take you to some of the most exciting areas to experience the real .

And of course you'll find all the practical tips you need for a smooth trip: itineraries for short visits, how to get around, and how much to tip the guy who serves you a drink at the end of a long day's exploration.

It's your guarantee of a really great experience.

Our Promise

You can trust our travel information because Lonely Planet authors visit the places we write about, each and every edition. We never accept freebies for positive coverage, so you can rely on us to tell it like it is.

QuickStart Guide 7

Explore London 21

Worth a Trip:

QuickStart Guide

Welcome to London

London has something for everyone, from art to grand museums, dazzling architecture, royalty, diversity, glorious parks and irrepressible pizazz. It's immersed in history, but London is also a tireless innovator of culture and creative talent, while a cosmopolitan dynamism makes it quite possibly the world's most international city, yet one that remains somehow intrinsically British.

St Paul's Cathedral (p88) and Millennium Bridge (p112)
KIMBERLEY COOLE/GETTY IMAGES ©

London
Top Sights

British Museum (p64)

With five million visitors annually, the British Museum is London's most popular tourist attraction – a vast and hallowed collection of artefacts, art and antiquity.

Tower of London (p84)

This fortress with its titanic stonework exudes a sense of ancient history at every turn. Few parts of the UK are as steeped in myth or as impregnated with legend.

St Paul's Cathedral (p88)

This astonishing church is world renowned, but only a visit to admire Sir Christopher Wren's masterful design, including a climb into the dome for some truly majestic views, can do it justice.

Tate Modern (p106)

Housed in a former power station, this modern art collection enjoys a triumphant position on the Thames. The Tate Modern is a vigorous statement of modernity and architectural renewal, and is incredibly popular.

National Gallery (p44)

This superlative collection of (largely premodern) art is one of the world's largest, featuring Leonardo da Vinci, Michelangelo, Turner, Monet, Renoir and Van Gogh in a superb building that dominates Trafalgar Sq.

Royal Observatory (p164)

Home to the Greenwich Meridian, the universal benchmark of time, and astronomical discoveries, the Royal Observatory combines history and science with great views of London and Greenwich Park.

Houses of Parliament (p30)

There's nothing as magnificent or more London than the sublime view of Big Ben and the Houses of Parliament from the River Thames.

Hampton Court Palace (p122)

Henry VIII's well-preserved Tudor palace, gardens and maze by the River Thames makes for a stunning escape from urban London. Put aside a day to do it justice.

Victoria & Albert Museum (p128)

You could virtually spend your entire trip in this magnificent South Kensington museum dedicated to the decorative arts and still be astounded by its variety and depth.

Natural History Museum (p132)

With its animatronic *T. rex*, towering Diplodocus skeleton, Wildlife Garden and Gothic fairy-tale architecture, this museum is a work of great curatorial imagination.

Westminster Abbey (p24)

Adorers of medieval ecclesiastic architecture will be in seventh heaven at this sublime abbey and sacred place of coronation for England's sovereigns. Get in the queue early.

Buckingham Palace (p28)

That the hoi polloi is able to breach (and tour) this imperious, blue-blooded bastion is remarkable. For royal enthusiasts, the palace is a superlative highlight of London.

Kew Gardens (p40)

An 18th-century 10-storey Chinese pagoda, a Japanese gateway, historic glasshouses, and a 17th-century royal palace sit in grounds among one of the world's most outstanding botanical collections.

London
Local Life

Insider tips to help you find the real cit

After checking out the top sights, get a more intimate sense of London and what makes it tick – explore the city's hip nightlife, its literary quarters, epic heathland, riverside charms, individual and striking shops, as well as its boho heritage.

A Stroll Through Soho (p46)

▶ Historic squares
▶ Creative vitality

At the heart of the West End, Soho's web of streets compresses culture, vitality, charm, shopping and diversity into a fascinating neighbourhood. Start in Chinatown and thread your way through historic squares, unique shops, back streets and markets to a drink in a celebrated Soho bar.

A Literary Walk Around Bloomsbury (p68)

▶ Georgian squares
▶ Literary heritage

Luminaries of the written word – Virginia Woolf, TS Eliot, Ted Hughes *et al* – have all left their mark on this part of London, leaving it indelibly associated with literary circles. Spend a day discovering the bookish charms of this elegant part of town, pausing to browse the shelves of one of the capital's finest bookshops for literary treasures, and concluding with a drink in a historic pub.

A Night out in Shoreditch (p102)

▶ Pubs and clubs
▶ Late-night snacking

Put sightseeing on hold as the sun sinks over Shoreditch for a fun and exuberant night out. This part of town fully comes alive in the evening, with gastropubs, clubs and converted Victorian drinking holes welcomin gregarious crowds and night owls looking for excitement on either side of the witching hour.

Shopping in Chelse & Knightsbridge (p136)

▶ Unique shops
▶ Art and architecture

The well-heeled streets of Chelsea and Knightsbridge harbour a select choice of shops for every one, from the bibliophile to those on the hunt for painfully stylish fashion accessories. Start by perusing the art collection of Charles Saatchi, glam up at Harvey Nichols an once you've shopped to your heart's content, dro in at a lovely local pub.

Soho Square (p47)

A Saturday in Notting Hill (p148)

▶ Market finds
▶ Stylish street life

Save a visit to Notting Hill for the weekend and catch the area at its best. Everything revolves around the lively hub of Portobello Market so make browsing and shopping your calling for the day, interlaced with some fine dining and a glass at one of the neighbourhood's best pubs.

Walking on Hampstead Heath (p160)

▶ Panoramic views
▶ Hampstead style

Desert the urban density of central London for the town's most famous heath. Start your journey in London's most sublime cemetery before climbing to wide-angle views over town and shopping for design wear in Hampstead village. Conclude your day with fine dining in a superb gastropub.

London
Day Planner

Day One

First stop, **Trafalgar Square** (p50) for its architectural grandeur and photo-op views of **Big Ben** (p31). Once you've had your fill of iconic landmarks, head indoors to the **National Gallery** (p44) to admire Van Gogh's *Sunflowers*. Head down **Whitehall**, where you'll pass the British Prime Minister's residence, **No 10 Downing St** (p36), before arriving at the magnificent **Houses of Parliament** (p30). Press on to **Westminster Abbey** (p24) and immerse yourself in history.

For gourmet cuisine at budget prices, head to the **Vincent Rooms** (p36) for lunch. Having recuperated, cross the river on **Westminster Bridge** to the **London Eye** (p113). Carry on along the south bank (or catch the RV1 bus to speed things up) to the **Tate Modern** (p106) for some A-grade art. Aim your camera at **St Paul's Cathedral** (p88) on the far side of the elegant **Millennium Bridge** (p112) and don't forget **Shakespeare's Globe** (p112).

Wind down with a drink in the historic **George Inn** (p118) off Borough High St and enjoy dinner at **Applebee's Fish Cafe** (p116) at the heart of the historic **Borough Market** (p121).

Day Two

Get to the **Tower of London** (p84) early (9am) to witness the **Ceremony of the Keys** and spend the morning following the beefeaters and marvelling at the **Crown Jewels**. When you're finished, take a minute to admire the iconic **Tower Bridge** (p94) on the Thames.

Make your way to **St Paul's Cathedral** (p88) to enjoy lunch in its wonderful crypt before taking an hour or so to admire the exquisite architecture. Hop on a bus to **Covent Garden** (p50) and take in the buzz around the piazza, shopping and admiring street performers. Continue to **Leicester Square** with its cinemas and film premieres and **Piccadilly Circus** (p50) and its famous statue.

After all this traipsing, head to **Opium** (p56) for a well-earned cocktail and follow it with divine dim sum at **Yauatcha** (p53) or delicious Beijing street classics at **Baozi Inn** (p55). Stay in Soho for the rest of the night, whether for cocktails at **LAB Soho** (p56) or a good ol' pint at the **White Horse** (p57).

Short on time?
We've arranged London's must-sees into these day-by-day itineraries to make sure you see the very best of the city in the time you have available.

Day Three

Devote a couple of hours to the **British Museum** (p64): download one of their brilliant one-hour **iPad tours** or join a free **EyeOpener tour** of the permanent collection before exploring under your own steam or visiting the fantastic temporary exhibitions. Round up the morning with a stroll around **Bloomsbury** (p68), the surrounding neighbourhood, once the undisputed centre of the literary world.

Have lunch at the **Newman Street Tavern** (p74), a delightful brasserie in nearby Fitzrovia, before heading to the upmarket borough of Chelsea and Kensington for an afternoon of retail therapy. Stop by **Harrods** (p147) or gourmet souvenirs, pop into **Harvey Nichols** (p137) for the latest beauty products and follow our recommendations of unique boutiques (p136). Round off the day with a stroll around **Hyde Park** (p140).

Come night, head to the buzzing nightlife of North London's **Camden**. Weekends, especially, are hopping. Settle down for some Caribbean delights at **Mango Room** (p156) before enjoying some live music. For indie rock, go to **Barfly** (p157); for jazz, make your way to **Blues Kitchen** (p157).

Day Four

Hop on a boat in central London and make your way to Greenwich with its fascinating history and fine riverside settings. Start your visit at the stunning **Cutty Sark** (p167), the only remaining clipper that sailed the seas during the 19th century tea trade years. Amble over to **Greenwich Market** (p169) for lunch and try one of the world cuisines from the market stalls.

Stroll through **Greenwich Park** (p167) all the way up to the **Royal Observatory** (p164). The views of **Canary Wharf**, the business district across the river, are stunning. Inside the Observatory, straddle the **Greenwich Meridian** and learn about the incredible quest to solve the longitude problem. At the **Planetarium**, join another quest: finding extra-terrestrial life. Walk back down to Greenwich and settle down for a pint at the **Trafalgar Tavern** (p169).

Head back to central London on the DLR from Greenwich and enjoy a typical London night out of drinking and clubbing in **Shoreditch** (p102).

Need to Know

**For more information,
see Survival Guide (p205)**

Currency
Pound sterling (£). 100 pence = £1

Language
English (and over 300 others)

Visas
Not required for US, Canadian, Australian, New Zealand or South African visitors for stays up to six months. European Union nationals can stay indefinitely.

Money
ATMs widespread. Major credit cards accepted everywhere.

Mobile Phones
Buy local SIM cards for European and Australian phones, or a pay-as-you-go phone. Set other phones to international roaming.

Time
London is on GMT; during British Summer Time (BST; late March to late October), London clocks are one hour ahead of GMT.

Plugs & Adaptors
Standard voltage is 230/240V AC, 50Hz. Three square pin plugs. Adaptors for European, Australasian and US electrical items are widely available.

Tipping
Round up to nearest pound or up to 10% for taxi drivers. Tip restaurant waiting staff between 10% and 15% if service isn't included.

① Before You Go

Your Daily Budget

Budget less than £80
► Dorm bed £10-30
► Market-stall lunch £5, supermarket sandwich £3-4
► Many museums free
► Standby theatre tickets £5-15
► Barclays bike daily charge £2

Midrange £80-180
► Double room £100-150
► Two-course dinner with glass of wine £30
► Theatre ticket £10-50

Top End over £180
► Four-star/boutique hotel room £200
► Three-course dinner in top restaurant with wine £60-90
► Black cab trip £30
► Top theatre ticket £65

Useful Websites

► **Lonely Planet** (www.lonelyplanet.com/london) Destination information, hotel bookings, great for planning.

► **Time Out** (www.timeout.com/london) Snappy, au courant London listings.

► **Londonist** (www.londonist.com) All about London and everything that happens in it.

Advance Planning

► **Three months** Book performances of top shows, a room at a popular hotel.

► **One month** Book tickets for fringe theatre, live music, festivals.

► **A few days** Check the weather on www.tfl.gov.uk/weather.

2 Arriving in London

Most visitors arrive at Heathrow Airport, 15 miles west of central London, or Gatwick Airport, 30 miles south of central London.

✈ From Heathrow Airport

Destination	Best Transport
Covent Garden	Underground or Heathrow Express then Underground
Kensington	Underground or Heathrow Express then Underground
Bloomsbury	Underground or Heathrow Express then Underground
The City	Underground or Heathrow Express then Underground
South Bank	Underground or Heathrow Express then Underground
Regent's Park & Camden	Underground or Heathrow Express then Underground

✈ From Gatwick Airport

Destination	Best Transport
Covent Garden	Gatwick Express then Underground
Kensington	Gatwick Express then Underground or easyBus
Bloomsbury	Gatwick Express then Underground
The City	Gatwick Express then Underground
South Bank	Train to London Bridge
Regent's Park & Camden	Train to King's Cross then Underground

3 Getting Around

Managed by Transport for London (www.tfl. gov.uk), public transport in London is excellent, if pricey. The Underground is the most convenient form of transport; the cheapest way to travel is with an Oyster Card.

⊖ Tube, Overground & DLR

The London Underground ('the tube'), Overground and DLR are, overall, the quickest and easiest ways to get about the city, if not the cheapest. The cheapest way to travel on the Underground is with an Oyster Card.

🚌 Bus

The bus network is extensive but slow-going except for short hops; fares are good value if used with an Oyster card and there are plentiful night buses and 24-hour routes.

🚗 Taxi

Black cab drivers always know where they are going, but fares are steep unless you're in a group. Minicabs are cheaper but must be booked in advance rather than flagged in the street. Fares are given at the time of booking.

🚲 Bicycle

Barclays Bikes are everywhere around central London and great for short hops.

🚗 Car & Motorcycle

As a visitor, it's unlikely you'll need to drive in London. Disincentives include extortionate parking charges, congestion charges, traffic jams, the high price of petrol, efficient traffic wardens and wheel clamps. But if that doesn't put you off, numerous car hire operations can be found across town from self-service, pay-as-you-drive vehicles to international firms (such as Avis and Hertz).

London
Neighbourhoods

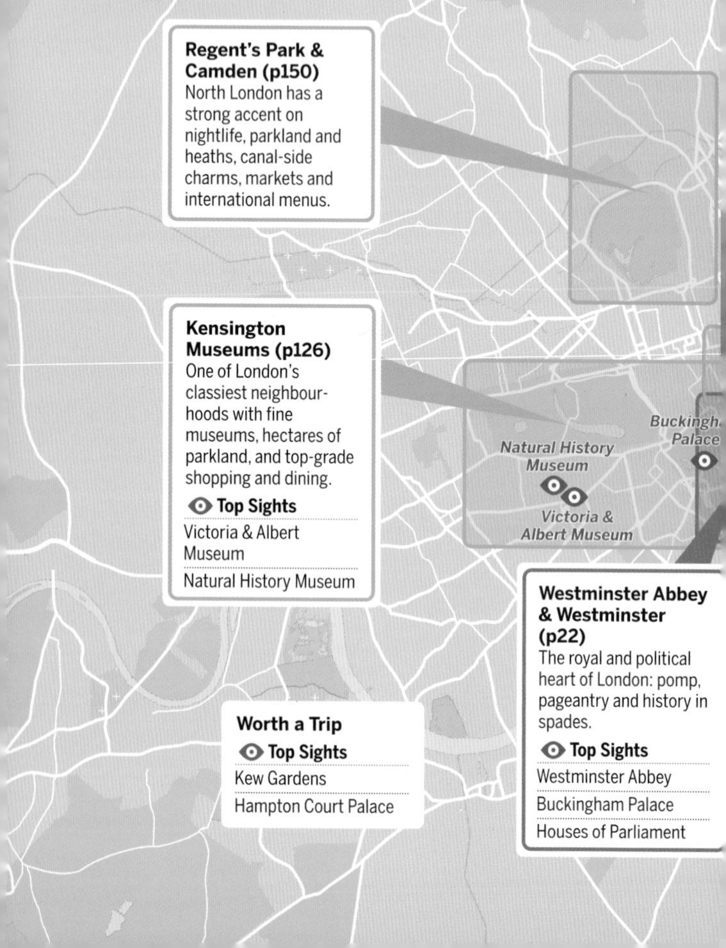

Regent's Park & Camden (p150)
North London has a strong accent on nightlife, parkland and heaths, canal-side charms, markets and international menus.

Kensington Museums (p126)
One of London's classiest neighbour-hoods with fine museums, hectares of parkland, and top-grade shopping and dining.

◎ Top Sights

Victoria & Albert Museum

Natural History Museum

Natural History Museum

Victoria & Albert Museum

Buckingha Palace

Westminster Abbey & Westminster (p22)
The royal and political heart of London: pomp, pageantry and history in spades.

◎ Top Sights

Westminster Abbey

Buckingham Palace

Houses of Parliament

Worth a Trip
◎ Top Sights
Kew Gardens

Hampton Court Palace

**British Museum &
Bloomsbury
(p62)**
London's most famous
museum, elegant
squares, eclectic dining
and literary pubs.

◉ **Top Sights**

British Museum

**National Gallery &
Covent Garden
(p42)**
Bright lights, big city:
West End theatres, big
ticket museums,
fantastic restaurants,
shopping galore and
boho nightlife.

◉ **Top Sights**

National Gallery

**St Paul's & the City
(p82)**
London's iconic church
and tower are here,
alongside ancient
remains, historic
churches, architectural
gems and hearty pubs.

◉ **Top Sights**

Tower of London

St Paul's Cathedral

ritish
useum

◉ St Paul's
Cathedral

◉ National
Gallery

◉ Tate
Modern

Tower of
London

◉ Houses of
Parliament

estminster
bey

**Tate Modern &
South Bank (p104)**
Modern art, innovative
theatre, Elizabethan
drama, superb dining,
modern architecture
and traditional pubs.

◉ **Top Sights**

Tate Modern

**The Royal
Observatory &
Greenwich (p162)**
Fine blend of grandeur
and village charm with
maritime history, a lively
market, great beer and
gorgeous parkland.

◉ **Top Sights**

Royal Observatory

◉ Royal
Observatory

Explore
London

Worth a Trip

View of London towards the Shard (p114)
TIM ROBBERTS/GETTY IMAGES ©

Explore

Westminster Abbey & Westminster

Westminster is the political heart of London, and the level of pomp and circumstance here is astounding – state occasions are marked by convoys of gilded carriages, elaborate parades and, in the case of the opening of Parliament, by a man in a black coat banging on the front door with a jewelled sceptre. Tourists flock here to marvel at Buckingham Palace and the neo-Gothic Houses of Parliament.

The Sights in a Day

☀ Get queuing at **Westminster Abbey** (p24) early in the day to thwart the crowds. You'll want to spend most of the morning here admiring its mighty stonework, exploring the cloisters and the Abbey's historic grandeur. Head to **St James's Park** (p34) for some greenery at lunchtime and choose between a picnic or a meal at the marvellous **Inn the Park** (p37).

☀ After lunch, choose between **Buckingham Palace** (p28) in summer (when the State Rooms are open) or the **Houses of Parliament** (p30) the rest of the year (when parliament is sitting). Alternatively, visit the **Churchill War Rooms** (p34) for a feel of what life in London was like during WWII.

☾ Dine at the **Vincent Rooms** (p36) for great cuisine at tiny prices before making your way to the West End to sample the astonishing range of bars, pubs, theatres, cinemas and clubs in the neighbouring National Gallery and Covent Garden area (p56).

 Top Sights

Westminster Abbey (p24)

Buckingham Palace (p28)

Houses of Parliament (p30)

♥ Best of London

Royal Sights

Buckingham Palace (p28)

Changing of the Guard (p34)

Horse Guards Parade (p35)

Banqueting House (p35)

Parks & Gardens

St James's Park (p34)

Green Park (p36)

Getting There

🚇 **Tube** Westminster and St James's Park are both on the Circle and District Lines. The Jubilee Line runs through Westminster and Green Park; the latter station is also visited by the Piccadilly and Victoria Lines.

Top Sights
Westminster Abbey

Adorers of medieval, ecclesiastic architecture will be in heaven at this sublime abbey and hallowed place of coronation for England's sovereigns. Almost every nook and cranny tells a story, but few sights in London are as beautiful, or as well-preserved, as the Henry VII Lady Chapel. Elsewhere you will find the oldest door in the UK, Poets' Corner, the Coronation Chair, 14th-century cloisters, a 900-year-old garden, royal sarcophagi and much more.

◉ Map p32, D4

☑ 020-7222 5152

www.westminster-abbey.org

20 Dean's Yard, SW1

adult/child £18/8, tours £3

🕑 9.30am-4.30pm Mon, Tue, Thu & Fri, to 7pm Wed, to 2.30pm Sat

Ⓔ Westminster

The Quire (p27) at Westminster Abbey

Don't Miss

North Transept

The north transept is often referred to as Statesmen's Aisle: politicians and eminent public figures are commemorated by staggeringly large marble statues and plaques. The Whig and Tory prime ministers who dominated late Victorian politics, Gladstone (who is buried here) and Disraeli (who is not), have their monuments uncomfortably close to one another.

Sanctuary

At the heart of the Abbey is the sanctuary, where coronations, royal weddings and funerals take place. George Gilbert Scott designed the ornate high altar in 1897. In front of the altar is a rare marble pavement dating back to 1268. It has intricate designs of small pieces of marble inlaid into plain marble.

Henry VII Lady Chapel

This spectacular chapel has a fan-vaulted ceiling, colourful heraldic banners and oak stalls. Behind the chapel's altar is the elaborate sarcophagus of Henry VII and his queen, Elizabeth of York. Opposite the entrance to the Lady Chapel is the Coronation Chair, seat of coronation for almost every monarch since the late 13th century.

Tomb of Mary, Queen of Scots

Two small chapels on either side of Lady Chapel contain the tombs of famous monarchs: on the left rest Elizabeth I and her half-sister 'Bloody Mary'. On the right lies Mary, Queen of Scots, beheaded on the orders of her cousin Elizabeth in cahoots with her son, the future James I.

☑ Top Tips

▶ Crowds are almost as solid as the Abbey's stonework, so get to the front of the queue first thing in the morning.

▶ Hop on one of the 90-minute tours led by vergers (£3) and departing from the north door.

▶ Grab an audioguide, free with your entry tickets at the north door.

✕ Take a Break

Get drinks and snacks at the **Coffee Club** in the Abbey's Great Cloister; for a sit-down meal head to **Cellarium** (☏ 020-7222 0516; www.cellariumcafe. com; mains £9.50-14.50; ⊘9am-6pm Mon-Fri, to 4.30pm Sat), part of the original 14th-century Benedictine monastery, with stunning views of the Abbey's architectural details.

Not far from the Abbey, the Vincent Rooms (p36) is great for top-notch modern European cuisine at rock-bottom prices.

Shrine of St Edward the Confessor

The most sacred spot in the Abbey lies behind the high altar; access is generally restricted to protect the 13th-century floor. St Edward was the founder of the Abbey and the original building was consecrated a few weeks before his death. His tomb was slightly altered after the original was destroyed during the Reformation.

Poets' Corner

The south transept contains Poets' Corner, where many of England's finest writers are buried and/or commemorated. The first poet to be buried here was Geoffrey Chaucer, joined later by Tennyson, Charles Dickens, Robert Browning, Rudyard Kipling and other greats.

Cloisters

Providing access to the monastic buildings, the quadrangular cloisters – dating largely from the 13th to 15th centuries – would once have been a very active part of the Abbey and busy with monks. The cloisters also provide access to the Chapter House, the Pyx Chamber and the Abbey Museum, situated in the vaulted undercroft.

Chapter House

The octagonal Chapter House has one of Europe's best-preserved medieval tile floors and retains traces of religious murals. Used as a meeting place by the House of Commons in the second half of the 14th century, it

also boasts what is claimed to be the oldest door in the UK – it's been there 950 years.

Pyx Chamber

Next to the Chapter House and off the East Cloister, the Pyx Chamber is one of the few remaining relics of the original Abbey and contains the Abbey's treasures and liturgical objects. Note the enormous trunks, which were made inside the room and used to store valuables from the exchequer.

Abbey Museum

Next door to the Pyx Chamber, this museum exhibits the death masks of generations of royalty, wax effigies representing Charles II and William III, as well as armour and stained glass.

College Garden

To reach the 900-year-old **College Garden** (⊙10am–6pm Tue-Thu Apr-Sep, to 4pm Tue-Thu Oct-Mar), enter Dean's Yard and the Little Cloisters off Great College St. It occupies the site of the Abbey's first infirmary garden for cultivating medicinal herbs, established in the 11th century.

Sir Isaac Newton's Tomb

On the western side of the cloister is Scientists' Corner, where you will find Sir Isaac Newton's tomb; a nearby section of the northern aisle of the nave is known as Musicians' Aisle, where baroque composers Henry Purcell and John Blow are buried.

Understand
History of Westminster Abbey
- -

Although a mixture of architectural styles, Westminster Abbey is considered the finest example of Early English Gothic (1180–1280). The original church was built in the 11th century by King (later St) Edward the Confessor, who is buried in the chapel behind the main altar. Henry III (r 1216–72) began work on the new building but didn't complete it; the French Gothic nave was finished in 1388. Henry VII's huge and magnificent chapel was added in 1519.

Benedictine Monastery & Dissolution
The Abbey was initially a monastery for Benedictine monks. Many of the building's features attest to this collegial past (the octagonal chapter room, the Quire and cloisters). In 1540, Henry VIII separated the Church of England from the Catholic Church and dissolved the monastery. The King became head of the Church of England and the Abbey acquired its 'royal peculiar' status (administered directly by the Crown and exempt from any ecclesiastical jurisdiction).

Site of Coronation
With the exception of Edward V and Edward VIII, every English sovereign since William the Conqueror (in 1066) has been crowned here, and most of the monarchs from Henry III (d 1272) to George II (d 1760) were also buried here.

The Quire
The Quire, a sublime structure of gold, blue and red Victorian Gothic by Edward Blore, dates back to the mid-19th century. It sits where the original choir for the monks' worship would have been but bears no resemblance to the original. The Westminster Choir still uses it regularly for singing.

Royal Wedding
On 29 April 2011, Prince William married Catherine Middleton at Westminster Abbey. The couple had chosen the Abbey for the relatively intimate setting of the Sanctuary – because of the Quire, three-quarters of the 1900 or so guests couldn't see a thing!

Top Sights
Buckingham Palace

The official residence of Her Royal Highness Queen Elizabeth II – Lilibet to those who know her – is a stunning piece of Georgian architecture, crammed with the kind of gold- and gem-encrusted chintz that royals like to surround themselves with. Built in 1705 as Buckingham House for the duke of the same name, the palace has been the Royal Family's London lodgings since 1837, when Queen Victoria moved in.

◉ Map p32, A4

☎ 020-7766 7300

www.royalcollection.org.uk

Buckingham Palace Rd, SW1

adult/child £19/10.85

◷ 9.30am-7pm late Jul-Aug, to 6.30pm Sep

◉ St James's Park, Victoria, Green Park

Buckingham Palace

Don't Miss

State Rooms

Visits start in the Grand Hall and take in the State Dining Room (all red damask and Regency furnishings); then move on to the Blue Drawing Room (with a gorgeous fluted ceiling by John Nash), the White Drawing Room, where foreign ambassadors are received, and the ballroom. The Throne Room displays his-and-hers pink chairs initialled 'ER' and 'P'.

Picture Gallery & Gardens

The 47m-long Picture Gallery features works by such artists as Van Dyck, Rembrandt, Canaletto, Poussin, Canova and Vermeer. Wandering the gardens is another highlight: admire some of the 350-or-so species of flowers and plants, get beautiful views of the palace and a peek at the lake.

Queen's Gallery

The Royal Family has amassed paintings, sculpture, ceramics, furniture and jewellery. The **Queen's Gallery** (www.royalcollection.org.uk; southern wing, Buckingham Palace, Buckingham Gate, SW1; adult/child £9.50/4.80, with Royal Mews £16.25/9.10; ☺10am-5.30pm; ☻St James's Park, Victoria, Green Park) showcases some of the palace's treasures on a rotating basis, through temporary exhibitions. Entrance to the gallery is through Buckingham Gate.

Royal Mews

A short walk southwest of Buckingham Palace, the **Royal Mews** (www.royalcollection.org.uk; Buckingham Palace Rd, SW1; adult/child £8/5, with Queen's Gallery £16.25/9.10; ☺10am-5pm Apr-Oct, to 4pm Mon-Sat Nov-Dec), once a falconry, is a working stable looking after the royals' horses, along with some opulent vehicles. Highlights include the magnificent gold coach of 1762 and the 1910 Glass Coach.

☑ Top Tips

▶ If bought direct from the palace ticket office, your ticket grants free re-admission to the palace for one year; simply have your ticket stamped on your first visit.

▶ The State Rooms are open only during August and September, when Her Majesty is holidaying in Scotland. The Queen's Gallery is open year-round and the Royal Mews from April to December.

▶ Audioguides are included in the ticket price for all tours.

▶ The Changing of the Guard is very popular; arrive early to secure a good view.

✗ Take a Break

Within the palace, the **Garden Café** on the West Terrace overlooks the lawn and lake.

In nearby St James's Park, Inn the Park (p37) offers both terrific British cuisine and great views.

Top Sights
Houses of Parliament

The House of Commons and House of Lords are housed in the sumptuous Palace of Westminster. The House of Commons is where Members of Parliament (MPs) meet to propose and discuss new legislation, and to grill the prime minister and other ministers. When Parliament is in session, visitors are allowed to attend debates in the House of Commons and the House of Lords. Even if you can't get inside, marvel at Sir Charles Barry's stunning building and its iconic tower.

◉ Map p32, E4

www.parliament.uk

Parliament Sq, SW1

admission free

Ⓔ Westminster

Houses of Parliament

Don't Miss

The Towers
The most famous feature of the Houses of Parliament is Elizabeth Tower, commonly known as **Big Ben**. Ben is the bell hanging inside and is named after Benjamin Hall, the commissioner of works when the tower was completed in 1858. Thirteen-tonne Ben has rung in the New Year since 1924.

Westminster Hall
One of the most stunning features of the Palace of Westminster, seat of the English monarchy from the 11th to the early 16th centuries, is Westminster Hall. The building was originally built in 1099; the roof was added between 1394 and 1401 and has been celebrated as 'the greatest surviving achievement of medieval English carpentry'.

House of Commons
The layout of the **Commons Chamber** (⊘2.30-10pm Mon & Tue, 11.30am-7.30pm Wed, 10.30am-6.30pm Thu, 9.30am-3pm Fri) is based on that of St Stephen's Chapel in the original Palace of Westminster. The current chamber, designed by Giles Gilbert Scott, replaced the one destroyed by a 1941 bomb.

House of Lords
The **House of Lords** (www.parliament.uk/business/lords; ⊘2.30-10pm Mon & Tue, 3-10pm Wed, 11am-7.30pm Thu, 10am to close of session Fri) can be visited via the 'Strangers' Gallery'. The Gothic interior led its architect, Pugin (1812–52), to an early death from overwork.

Tours
On Saturdays and when Parliament is in recess, visitors can join a 75-minute **guided tour** (☑0844 847 1672; www.ticketmaster.co.uk/housesofparliament; 75min tours adult/child £15/6) of both chambers, Westminster Hall and other historic buildings.

☑ Top Tips

▶ The best time to watch a debate is during Prime Minister's Question Time at noon Wednesday, but it's also the busiest.

▶ To find out what's being debated on a particular day, check the noticeboard beside the entrance, or online at www.parliament.uk.

▶ It's not unusual to have to wait up to two hours to access the chambers, so give yourself time.

✕ Take a Break

The **Jubilee Café** (⊘10am-5.30pm Mon-Fri, 10am-6pm Sat) near the north door of Westminster Hall serves hot drinks and snacks.

For delicious, seasonal British food, amble down to Inn the Park (p37), a fabulous wood-clad restaurant in the middle of St James's Park.

River Thames

Lambeth Bridge

Archbishop's Park

Millbank

Great College St

1 Tate Britain

Atterbury St

John Islip St

Herrick St

Erasmus St

Millbank

Tufton St

Marsham St

Dean's Yard

Great Smith St

Marsham St

Horseferry Rd

WESTMINSTER

Monck St

Page St

Vincent St

Regency St

Great Peter St

Medway St

Chadwick St

Regency St

Chapter St

Douglas St

Hide Pl

Broad Sanctuary

Old Pye St

Greycoat St

Elverton St

Vincent St

Maunsel St

Vincent Sq

Vauxhall Bridge Rd

Broad

Caxton St

Greycoat Pl

Rochester Row

Vincent Sq

Westminster School Playing Field

Vincent Sq

Tachbrook St

Victoria St

Howick Pl

Francis St

Greencoat Pl

Stillington St

Charlwood St

Belgrave Rd

ham Gate

Castle La

Stag Pl

Ashley Pl

Morpeth Tce

Willow Pl

Wilton Rd

Wilfred St

Carlisle Pl

Palace St

BressendenPl

Allington St

Victoria St Vauxhall Bridge Rd

Wilton Rd

Gillingham St

Bridge Pl

Ⓜ Victoria

For reviews see	
Ⓞ Top Sights	p24
Ⓞ Sights	p34
Ⓧ Eating	p36
Ⓧ Entertainment	p37
Ⓐ Shopping	p38

200 m
0.1 miles

Sights

Tate Britain
GALLERY

 1 Map p32, E8

The older and more venerable of the two Tates, this riverside Portland stone edifice celebrates British painting from 1500 to the present, with works from Blake, Hogarth, Gainsborough, Barbara Hepworth, Whistler, Constable and (in particular) Turner. It doesn't stop there: vibrant modern and contemporary art finds expression in works by Lucian Freud, Francis Bacon and Tracey Emin. (www.tate.org.uk; Millbank, SW1; admission free; ⊘10am-6pm daily, to 10pm some Fri; ⊖Pimlico)

Churchill War Rooms
MUSEUM

 2 Map p32, D3

Winston Churchill coordinated the Allied resistance against Nazi Germany on a Bakelite telephone from this underground military HQ during WWII. The Cabinet War Rooms remain much as they were when the lights were flicked off in 1945, capturing the drama and dogged spirit of the time, while the multimedia Churchill Museum provides intriguing insights into the resolute, cigar-smoking wartime leader. (www.iwm.org.uk/visits/churchill-war-rooms; Clive Steps, King Charles St, SW1; adult/child £17/free; ⊘9.30am-6pm, last entry 5pm; ⊖Westminster)

Changing of the Guard
CEREMONY

 3 Map p32, A4

At 11.30am daily from May to July (on alternate days weather permitting from August to March), the old guard (Foot Guards of the Household Regiment) comes off duty to be replaced by the new guard on the forecourt of Buckingham Palace. ighly popular, the show lasts about half an hour (brace for crowds). (Buckingham Palace Rd, Buckingham Palace, SW1; ⊖St James's Park, Victoria)

St James's Park
PARK

4 Map p32, C4

At just 23 hectares, St James's is one of the smallest but most groomed of London's royal parks. It has brilliant views of the London Eye, Westminster, St James's Palace, Carlton House Tce and Horse Guards Parade; the sight of Buckingham Palace from the footbridge spanning the central lake is photo-perfect and the best you'll find. (www.royalparks.gov.uk; The Mall, SW1; deckchairs per hr/day £1.50/7; ⊘5am-midnight, deckchairs Mar-Oct daylight hours; ⊖St James's Park, Green Park)

☑️ Top Tip

Tate to Tate Boat

The ultra-handy and colourful **Tate Boat** (one-way adult £5) links the Tate Britain to the Tate Modern every 40 minutes from 10.17am to 5.04pm.

DAVID C TOMLINSON/GETTY IMAGES ©

Horse Guards Parade

Horse Guards Parade HISTORIC SITE

5 👁 Map p32, D2

In a more accessible version of
the Changing of the Guard, the
mounted troops of the Household
Cavalry change guard here daily, at
the official vehicular entrance to the
royal palaces. A slightly less pompous
version takes place at 4pm, when the
dismounted guards are changed. On
the Queen's official birthday (June),
the Trooping of the Colour is staged
here. (www.changing-the-guard.com/london-
programme.html; Horse Guards Parade, off
Whitehall, W1; ⏱11am Mon-Sat, 10am Sun;
🚇Westminster, St James's Park)

Banqueting House PALACE

6 👁 Map p32, E2

This is the only surviving part of the
Tudor Whitehall Palace (1532), which
once stretched most of the way down
Whitehall and burned down in 1698.
Designed by Inigo Jones in 1622,
Banqueting House was England's
first purely Renaissance building and
looked like no other structure in the
country at the time. Apparently, the
English initially hated it. (www.hrp.org.
uk/BanquetingHouse; Whitehall, SW1; adult/
child £5/free; ⏱10am-5pm; 🚇Westminster)

Understand
No 10 Downing Street

It's charming that the official seat of the British prime minister is a bog-standard Georgian **townhouse** (www.number10.gov.uk; 10 Downing St, W1; Westminster) in Whitehall. Unless you have permission to file a petition, however, the closest you'll get to the famous black door is the gate on Whitehall (south of Banqueting House on the other side of the road).

St James's Palace   PALACE

7 ◉ Map p32, B2

The striking Tudor gatehouse of St James's Palace, the only surviving part of a building initiated by the palace-mad Henry VIII in 1530, is best approached from St James's St to the north of St James's Park. This was the official residence of kings and queens for more than three centuries. (www.royal.gov.uk/theroyalresidences/stjamesspalace/stjamesspalace.aspx; Cleveland Row, SW1; ⊖Green Park)

Royal Academy of Arts   GALLERY

8 ◉ Map p32, B1

Britain's oldest society devoted to the fine arts was founded in 1768 but the organisation moved to Burlington House exactly a century later. The collection contains drawings, paintings, architectural designs, photographs and sculptures by past and present academicians such as Joshua Reynolds, John Constable, Thomas Gainsborough, JMW Turner, David Hockney and Norman Foster. (www.royalacademy.org.uk; Burlington House, Piccadilly, W1; adult/child £10/6; ⊘10am-6pm Sat-Thu, to 10pm Fri; ⊖Green Park)

Take a Break Treat yourself to afternoon tea at the Wolseley (p37).

Green Park   PARK

9 ◉ Map p32, A2

Less manicured than other central London parks, 19-hectare Green Park has huge oaks and rarely feels overcrowded. It was once a duelling ground and, like Hyde Park, served as a vegetable garden during WWII. (www.royalparks.gov.uk; ⊘24hr; ⊖Green Park)

Eating

Vincent Rooms   MODERN EUROPEAN £

10 ✕ Map p32, C6

Care to be a guinea pig for student chefs at Westminster Kingsway College, where Jamie Oliver was trained? Service is eager to please, the atmosphere in the Brasserie and the Escoffier Room smarter than expected, and the food (including veggie options) ranges from wonderful to exquisite – at prices that put other culinary stars to shame. (☎020-7802 8391; www.thevincentrooms.com; Westminster Kingsway College, Vincent Sq, SW1; mains £8-12; ⊘noon-2pm Mon-Fri, 6-8pm Wed & Thu; ⊖Victoria)

Inn the Park
BRITISH ££

 11 Map p32, C3

This stunning wooden cafe and restaurant in St James's Park is run by Irish wonderchef Oliver Peyton and offers cakes and tea, plus excellent British food, with the menu changing monthly. The terrace, which overlooks the park's fountains with views of Whitehall's grand buildings, is wonderful in warm weather. (020-7451 9999; www. innthepark.com; St James's Park, SW1; mains £14.50-22.50; 8am-6pm Oct-Mar, 8am-11pm Apr-Sep; Charing Cross, St James's Park)

Wolseley
MODERN EUROPEAN £££

12 Map p32, A1

This Bentley car showroom has been transformed into a Viennese-style brasserie, with chandeliers and black-and-white tiled floors, and remains a great place for spotting celebrities. That said, the Wolseley tends to work better for breakfast, brunch or tea, rather than lunch or dinner, when the dishes (such as Wiener schnitzel and *choucroute à l'Alsacienne* – sauerkraut with sausages and charcuterie) are somewhat stodgy. (020-7499 6996; www.thewolseley.com; 160 Piccadilly, W1; mains £10-36; 7am-midnight Mon-Fri, 8am-midnight Sat, 8am-11pm Sun; Green Park)

Mint Leaf
INDIAN ££

13 Map p32, C1

This large, very central place just up from Trafalgar Sq represents a new breed of Indian restaurant – all sleek design and a highly inventive menu. Dishes come in large and small sizes – a boon for a couple anxious to sample a few – and the vegetarian options are bountiful. Set lunch of two/three courses is £14/18. (020-7930 9020; www. mintleafrestaurant.com; Suffolk Pl, Haymarket, SW1; mains £16-23; noon-3pm Mon-Fri, 5.30-11pm daily; ; Piccadilly Circus)

Entertainment

Institute of Contemporary Arts
ARTS CENTRE

 14 Map p32, D2

Housed in a John Nash building along the Mall, the nontraditional ICA is where Picasso and Henry Moore had their first UK shows. Since then the ICA has been on the cutting (and controversial) edge of the British arts world, with an excellent range of experimental and progressive films, music nights, photography, art,

Top Tip
Westminster Nightlife?
Westminster and Whitehall are totally deserted in the evenings, with little in the way of bars or restaurants. It's pretty much the same story for St James's. If you find yourself in Westminster in the early evening, head north to vibrant Soho for fantastic bars and restaurants, or to the lively streets surrounding Covent Garden.

lectures, multimedia works and book readings. (ICA; ☎020-7930 9493; www.ica.org.uk; Nash House, The Mall, SW1; admission free; ☺11am-11pm Tue-Sun, exhibition times vary; 🛜; ⊖Charing Cross)

Shopping

Fortnum & Mason DEPARTMENT STORE

15 🔒 Map p32, B1

London's oldest grocery store, now into its fourth century, refuses to yield to modern times. Its staff are still dressed in old-fashioned tailcoats and it keeps its glamorous food hall supplied with hampers, cut marmalade, special teas and so on. Downstairs is an elegant wine bar, as well as elegant kitchenware, luxury gifts and perfumes. (www.fortnumandmason.com; 181 Piccadilly, W1; ☺10am-8pm Mon-Sat, 11.30am-6pm Sun; ⊖Piccadilly Circus)

Understand
Smash & Grab

Burlington Arcade was the scene of a dramatic robbery in June 1964, when a Jaguar Mark 10 sped along the narrow arcade before disgorging masked men who then made off with £35,000 worth of jewellery from the Goldsmiths and Silversmiths Association shop. The Jaguar – the only car to have ever driven down the arcade – then reversed back up the arcade and sped off.

Burlington Arcade SHOPPING ARCADE

16 🔒 Map p32, B1

This delightful arcade, which was built in 1819, is a shopping precinct for the wealthy and is most famous for the Burlington Berties, uniformed guards who patrol the area keeping an eye out for such offences as running, chewing gum or whatever else might lower the tone. (www.burlington-arcade.co.uk; 51 Piccadilly, W1; ☺10am-9pm Mon-Fri, 9am-6.30pm Sat, 11am-5pm Sun; ⊖Green Park)

Penhaligon's ACCESSORIES

17 🔒 Map p32, A1

Penhaligon's is the antidote to buying your favourite scent at airport duty-free. Here attendants ask about your favourite smells, take you on an exploratory tour of the shop's signature range and help you discover new scents. There is a range of products, from traditional perfumes to home fragrances and bath and body products. Everything's made in Cornwall. (www.penhaligons.com; 16-17 Burlington Arcade, W1; ☺10am-6pm Mon-Fri, to 6.30pm Sat, 11am-5pm Sun; ⊖Piccadilly Circus, Green Park)

Dover Street Market CLOTHING

18 🔒 Map p32, A1

Showcasing the colourful creations of Tokyo fashion darlings Comme des Garçons (among other labels), Dover St Market is the place to come for that shirt you only wear on special occasions. There are four floors of clothing for men and women, all artfully displayed. (www.doverstreetmarket.com; 17-18 Dover St, W1; ⊘11am-6.30pm Mon-Wed, to 7pm Thu-Sat, noon-5pm Sun; ⊖Green Park)

Taylor of Old Bond Street

BEAUTY

19 🔒 Map p32, B1

This shop has been plying its trade since the mid-19th century and has contributed much to the idea of 'the well-groomed gentleman'. It stocks every sort of razor, shaving brush and scent of shaving soap imaginable – not to mention oils, soaps and other bath products. (www.tayloroldbondst.co.uk; 74 Jermyn St, SW1; ⊘9am-6pm Mon-Sat; ⊖Green Park)

Shepherds

GIFTS

20 🔒 Map p32, B7

Suckers for fine stationery, leather boxes, elegant albums and exquisite paper will get their fix at this tiny shop in a wonderful bookbindery. (www.bookbinding.co.uk; 76 Rochester Row, SW1; ⊘10am-7pm Tue-Fri, to 8pm Sat; ⊖Victoria)

Minamoto Kitchoan

FOOD

21 🔒 Map p32, B1

Walking into this Japanese sweet shop is a mind-blowing experience.

CHRISTER FREDRIKSSON/GETTY IMAGES ©

Burlington Arcade

Wagashi – Japanese sweets – are made out of all sorts of rice and sweet red-bean paste *(anko)* and shaped into glazed red cherries, green-bean bunches or spiky kidney bean rolls. Order a couple, sit down and enjoy with a complimentary green tea, or buy a box as a gift. (www.kitchoan.com; 44 Piccadilly, W1; ⊘10am-7pm Sun-Fri, to 8pm Sat; ⊖Piccadilly Circus)

Top Sights
Kew Gardens

Getting There

⊖ Kew Gardens
(District line).

🚃 National Rail serv-
ices run from Waterloo
to Kew Bridge station.
The Overground stops
at Kew Gardens.

⛴ Arrive by ferry
(www.wpsa.co.uk).

The 121-hectare gardens at Kew are the finest prod-
uct of the British botanical imagination and really
should not be missed. As well as being a public garden, Kew is a pre-eminent research centre, with the
largest collection of plants in the world. No worries
if you don't know your golden slipper orchid from
your fengoky or your quiver tree from your alang-
alang, a visit to Kew is a journey of discovery for
everyone.

Palm House, Kew Gardens

Don't Miss

Palm House
The enormous and iconic Palm House, a domed hothouse of metal and 700 curved sheets of glass dating from 1848, houses a splendid display of exotic tropical greenery; the aerial walkway offers a parrots'-eye view of the lush vegetation.

Princess of Wales Conservatory
Further north, this stunning conservatory houses plants in 10 different climatic zones – everything from a desert to a mangrove swamp.

Temperate House
The beautiful Temperate House (north of the pagoda) is the world's largest surviving Victorian glasshouse, an astonishing feat of architecture housing an equally sublime collection of plants.

Rhizotron & Xstrata Treetop Walkway
In the Arboretum – a short walk from Temperate House – this fascinating and much-enjoyed walkway takes you underground and then 18m into the tree canopy.

Kew Palace
Red-brick **Kew Palace** (www.hrp.org.uk/kewpalace; ⏰9.30am-5.30pm Apr-Sep) in the northwest of the gardens is a former royal residence, built in 1631. Don't miss the restored Georgian rooms and Princess Elizabeth's wonderful doll's house.

Chinese Pagoda
Kew's celebrated 163ft tall, eight-sided Chinese Pagoda (1762), designed by William Chambers (who designed Somerset House), is one of the garden's architectural icons.

www.kew.org.uk

Kew Rd

adult/child £16/free

⏰9.30am-6.30pm Apr-Aug, earlier closing other months

🚢Kew Pier, 🚆Kew Bridge, 🚇Kew Gardens

☑ Top Tips
▶ Hop on and off the gardens' **Kew Explorer** (adult/child £4/2).

▶ Kids can explore the **Treehouse Towers** and **Climbers and Creepers**.

✕ Take a Break
Excellent cafe the **Orangery** is in a grade-1-listed 18th-century building near Kew Palace. Outside the gardens, **Glasshouse** (☎020-8940 6777; www.glasshouserestaurant.co.uk; 14 Station Pde, TW9; 3-course lunch £27.50-32.50, 3-course dinner £42.50; ⏰noon-2.30pm & 6.30-10.30pm Mon-Sat, 12.30-3pm & 7-10pm Sun; 🚻; 🚆Kew Gardens, 🚇Kew Gardens) is the perfect conclusion to a day of exploring.

Explore

National Gallery & Covent Garden

At the centre of the West End – London's physical, cultural and social heart – the neighbourhood around the National Gallery and Covent Garden is a sightseeing hub. This is London's busiest area, with a grand convergence of monumental history, stylish restaurants, standout entertainment choices and pubs. And if you're in town to shop, you'll be in seventh heaven here.

The Sights in a Day

 Start with the **National Gallery** (p44), but aim for a selective tour of your favourite artists. **Trafalgar Square** (p50) is perfect for a break and sublime views, and the **National Portrait Gallery** (p50) has some outstanding exhibits. Lunch can be expediently supplied by the splendid **National Dining Rooms** (p45) in the Sainsbury Wing of the National Gallery.

Walk off your meal, heading east along The Strand to browse around **Covent Garden Piazza** (p50), shopping, exploring and watching the street performers. The **London Transport Museum** (p52) is excellent, especially if you're with kids.

Have a table booked at **Yauatcha** (p53) for superb dim sum, or brave the queues for authentic Indian fare at **Dishoom** (p52). If post-dinner drinks are in order, go for a cocktail at **Opium** (p56), otherwise buy tickets for a West End musical, theatre or opera to round off the night.

For a local's day in Covent Garden and Soho, see p46.

 Top Sights

National Gallery (p44)

 Local Life

A Stroll Through Soho (p46)

 Best of London

Eating
Yauatcha (p53)

Bocca di Lupo (p55)

Dishoom (p52)

Gay & Lesbian
Edge (p57)

Candy Bar (p57)

Heaven (p57)

Entertainment
Royal Opera House (p58)

Ronnie Scott's (p58)

Getting There

◉ **Tube** Piccadilly Circus, Leicester Sq and Covent Garden (all Piccadilly Line) or Leicester Sq, Charing Cross and Embankment (all Northern Line).

Top Sights
National Gallery

With more than 2000 Western European paintings on display, this is one of the largest galleries in the world, although it's the quality rather than quantity of the works that impresses most. There are seminal paintings from every important epoch in the history of art from the mid-13th to the early 20th century, including works by Leonardo da Vinci, Michelangelo, Titian, Van Gogh and Renoir.

◉ Map p48, E5

www.nationalgallery.
org.uk

Trafalgar Sq, WC2

admission free

🕙10am-6pm Sat-Thu, to 9pm Fri

⊖Charing Cross

Rokeby Venus by Velázquez, National Gallery

Don't Miss

Sainsbury Wing
The Sainsbury Wing (1260–1510) houses plenty of fine religious paintings commissioned for private devotion, as well as more unusual masterpieces such as Botticelli's *Venus & Mars*.

West Wing & North Wing
The High Renaissance (1510–1600) is covered in the West Wing with Michelangelo, Correggio, El Greco and Bronzino, while Rubens, Rembrandt and Caravaggio are in the North Wing (1600–1700). There are two self-portraits of Rembrandt and the beautiful *Rokeby Venus* by Velázquez.

East Wing
The East Wing (1700–1900) houses a magnificent collection of 18th-century British landscape artists such as Gainsborough, Constable and Turner, and impressionist and post-Impressionist masterpieces by Van Gogh and Monet.

Rain, Steam & Speed: The Great Western Railway
ROOM 34

This magnificent oil painting from Turner was created in 1844. Generally considered to depict the Maidenhead Railway Bridge, the painting reveals the forces reshaping the world at the time: railways, speed and a reinterpretation of the use of light, atmosphere and colour in art.

Sunflowers
ROOM 45

One of several Sunflower still lifes painted by the artist in late 1888, this Van Gogh masterpiece displays a variety of then innovative artistic techniques, while the saturating vividness of the colour conveys a powerful sense of affirmation.

☑ Top Tips

▶ Free one-hour introductory guided tours leave from the information desk in the Sainsbury Wing daily at 11.30am and 2.30pm, and at 7pm on Friday.

▶ Aim for late night visits on Friday, when the gallery is open till 9pm.

▶ There are children's trails and activity sheets.

▶ The comprehensive audioguide (£3.50) is highly recommended.

✕ Take a Break

For sustenance, look no further than the **National Dining Rooms** (Map p48, E5; ☎020-7747 2525; www.peytonandbyrne. co.uk; 1st fl, Sainsbury Wing, National Gallery, Trafalgar Sq, WC2 ; mains £15.50-20.50; ⏱10am-5.30pm Sat-Thu, till 8.30pm Fri; ⊖Charing Cross), run by Irish chef Oliver Peyton and providing high-quality British food and an all-day bakery.

Portrait (p53) in the National Portrait Gallery blends fine food with fine views.

Local Life
A Stroll Through Soho

Soho may come into its own in the evenings, but daytime guarantees other surprises and opportunities to be charmed by the area's bohemian and bookish leanings, vitality, diversity, architectural narratives and creative energy. Thread your way from Chinatown through intriguing backstreets, genteel squares and street markets to one of the neighbourhood's signature bars.

❶ Explore Chinatown

Just north of Leicester Sq tube station are Lisle and Gerrard Sts, the focal point for London's Chinese community. A tight tangle of supermarkets, roast-duck houses and dim sum canteens, London's Chinatown isn't as big as Chinatowns in many other cities, but it's bubbly and indelibly Cantonese in flavour.

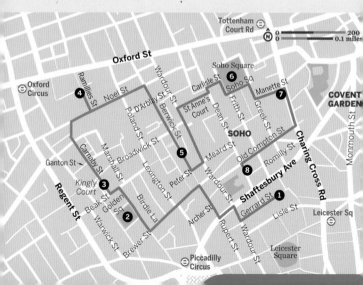

❷ Relax in Golden Square

North of Brewer St, historic Golden Sq – featured in Charles Dickens' *The Life and Adventures of Nicholas Nickleby* – was once part of an area called Windmill Fields. This lovely 17th century square was in all probability Christopher Wren's design; the garden in the middle is a relaxing place to find a bench.

❸ Designer Shopping on Carnaby Street

Pedestrian Carnaby St (and the handful of streets fanning off it) is a haven for brands and designer boutiques. All the big names – from M.A.C. to Miss Sixty, Levi's to The North Face – have shops here and the crowds never seem to thin.

❹ Visit the Photographers' Gallery

The fantastic **Photographers' Gallery** (www.photonet.org.uk; 16-18 Ramillies St, W1; admission free; ⏰10am-6pm Mon-Wed, Fri & Sat, to 8pm Thu, 11.30am-6pm Sun; ⊖Oxford Circus) has three floors of exhibition space, a new cafe and a shop brimming with photography-related goodies. It awards the prestigious annual Deutsche Börse Photography Prize; past winners include Andreas Gursky, Boris Mikhailov and Juergen Teller.

❺ Pick up Picnic Supplies in Berwick Street Market

Berwick Street Market (Berwick St , W1; ⏰9am-6pm Mon-Sat; ⊖Piccadilly Circus, Oxford Circus) has been here since the 1840s and is a great place to put together a picnic or shop for a prepared meal. Berwick St is famously the location of the Oasis album cover *(What's the Story) Morning Glory?*

❻ Stopover in Soho Square

Cut through tiny St Anne's Ct to Dean St (where Karl Marx and family lived between 1851–56, at No 28). Leafy Soho Sq beyond is where people come to laze in the sun on warm days. Laid out in 1681, it was originally named King's Sq (hence the statue of Charles II in its northern half).

❼ Browse Foyles

Even the most obscure titles await discovery at **Foyles** (www.foyles.co.uk; 113-119 Charing Cross Rd, WC2; ⏰9.30am-9pm Mon-Sat, 11.30am-6pm Sun; ⊖Tottenham Court Rd), London's legendary bookshop and a vast Charing Cross Rd institution since 1903. The lovely cafe is on the 1st floor and Ray's Jazz Shop is up on the 5th floor.

❽ Quaff Wine in French House

Walk down Old Compton St to Soho's legendary boho boozer, **French House** (www.frenchhousesoho.com; 49 Dean St, W1; ⏰noon-11pm Mon-Sat, to 10.30pm Sun; ⊖Leicester Sq), the meeting place of Free French Forces during WWII; de Gaulle is said to have drunk here often, while Dylan Thomas, Peter O'Toole and Francis Bacon frequently ended up horizontal.

A
B
C
D

1

Mortimer St

Riding Wells St

Little Portland St

Gresse St

Great Russell St

Margaret St

Great Titchfield St

Berners St

Newman St

Rathbone Pl

Hanway St

Tottenham Court Rd

Perry's Pl

Oxford St

Tottenham Court Rd

Eastcastle St

Great Portland St

Winsley St

2

Oxford Circus

Oxford St

Ramillies St

Poland St

Noel St

Berwick St

Wardour St

Great Chapel St

25 🟢

Sutton Row

Soho Sq

Frith St

32 ⭐

Manette St

Greek St

Great Marlborough St

Poland St

D'Arblay St

40 🔒

St Anne's Court

26 🟢

30 ⭐

Dean St

31 ⭐

21 🟢

39 🔒

29 ⭐

43 🔒

33 ⭐

Berwick St Market

37 🔒

13 ❌

Broadwick St

14 ❌ 15 ❌

Ingestre Pl

Peter St

Meard St

Old Compton St

SOHO

Shaftesbury Ave

Kingly St

Ganton St

Carnaby St

Marshall St

Beak St

Lexington St

Wardour St

19 🟢

Gerrard St

36 🔒

Kingly Court

Birdie La

Brewer St

Great Windmill St

24 🟢

17 🟢

Rupert St

Archer St

Leicester

Golden Sq

11 ❌

Warwick St

Sherwood St

Denman St

12 ❌

Glasshouse St

Piccadilly Circus

Oxendon St

Leicester Sq

Leices Squa

28 ⭐

Panton St

Clifford St

Heddon St

Regent St

42 🔒

3 🟢

Piccadilly Circus

Haymarket

Whitcom

Regent St

Piccadilly

Jermyn St

St Alban's St

Suffolk St

Eagle Pl

38 🔒

St James's St

Charles II St

Pall Ma

Duke of York St

Regent St

ST JAMES'S

For reviews see	
🟢 Top Sights	p44
🟢 Sights	p50
❌ Eating	p52
🟢 Drinking	p56
🔒 Entertainment	p58
🔒 Shopping	p60

E

F

G

H

Bloomsbury St

Museum St

New Oxford St

High Holborn

Holborn

HOLBORN

New Oxford St

Bucknall St

Grape St

High Holborn

Newton St

Whetstone Park

Lincoln's
Inn Fields

Sir John
Soane's
Museum
6

St Giles High St

Drury La

Stukely St

Macklin St

Parker St

Great Queen St

Wild Ct

Kingsway

Lincoln's
Inn Fields

Endell St

Shorts Gardens

Sardinia St

New Compton St

Neal St

Betterton St

16

COVENT
GARDEN

Wild St

Shelton St

Shaftesbury Ave

Monmouth St

Earlham St

Long Acre

Drury La

Russell St

Kemble St

Kean St

2

Flower
Market

Neal St

Broad Ct

Crown Ct

Wellington St

Catherine St

Tavistock St

Aldwych

West St

Langley St

Bow St

3

Litchfield St

Mercer St

Covent
Garden
Piazza
27

The Strand

Charing Cross Rd

10

Long Acre

James St

Floral St

4

41

8
London
Transport
Museum

Bow St

35

Covent Garden

Exeter St

Courtauld
Gallery
7

Rose St

20

King St

Somerset
House
5

Leicester Sq

Garrick St

Henrietta St

Southampton St

Tavistock St

Lancaster Pl

New Row

Bedfordbury

Maiden La

Savoy St

St Martin's La

Chandos Pl

Bedford St

Carting La

Savoy Pl

National
Portrait
Gallery
2

34

William IV St

Strand

John Adam St

Adam St

Victoria Embankment

National
Gallery

St Martin-
in-the-
Fields
9

Villiers St

Victoria
Embankment
Gardens

River Thames

Trafalgar
Square
1

23

22
Charing Cross

Craven St

N 0
0

200 m
0.1 miles

Sights

Trafalgar Square SQUARE

1 ⊙ Map p48, E5

This grand piazza commemorates the victory of the Royal Navy at the Battle of Trafalgar against the French and Spanish navies in 1805. The 52m-high **Nelson's Column** honours Lord Admiral Horatio Nelson, who led the fleet's victory over Napoleon. The four enormous **bronze lion statues** were sculpted by Sir Edwin Landseer and cast with seized Spanish and French cannons. (WC2; ⊖Charing Cross)

National Portrait Gallery GALLERY

2 ⊙ Map p48, E5

The fascinating National Portrait Gallery is like stepping into a picture book of English history. Founded in 1856, the permanent collection starts with the Tudors on the 2nd floor and descends to contemporary figures (from pop stars to scientists). An audiovisual guide (£3) will lead you through the gallery's 200 most famous pictures. (www.npg.org.uk; St Martin's Pl, WC2; admission free; ◷10am-6pm Sat-Wed, to 9pm Thu & Fri; ⊖Charing Cross, Leicester Sq)

Take a Break Portrait (p53), on the gallery's 3rd floor, offers outstanding food and views.

Piccadilly Circus SQUARE

3 ⊙ Map p48, C4

Piccadilly Circus is buzzing with the liveliness that makes London exciting. At the centre is the famous aluminium statue, known as the Angel of Christian Charity, dedicated to the philanthropist and child-labour abolitionist Lord Shaftesbury. The angel has been mistaken for Eros, the God of Love, but actually depicts Anteros, his twin brother. (⊖Piccadilly Circus)

Covent Garden Piazza SQUARE

4 ⊙ Map p48, G3

London's first planned square is now the preserve of tourists, who flock here to shop in the old arcades and be entertained by street performers. On its western flank is St Paul's Church. Check out the lovely courtyard at the back of the church, perfect for a picnic. (www.coventgardenlondonuk.com/-/covent-garden-piazza; ⊖Covent Garden)

Somerset House HISTORIC BUILDING

5 ⊙ Map p48, H4

With its 55 dancing fountains, this splendid Palladian masterpiece was designed by William Chambers in 1775 for royal societies and now contains the Courtauld Gallery (p51), a standout gallery connected to the Courtauld Institute of Arts; the **Embankment Galleries** host regular photographic exhibitions. (www.somersethouse.org.uk; The Strand, WC2; ◷galleries 10am-6pm, Safra Courtyard 7.30am-11pm; ⊖Charing Cross, Embankment, Temple)

Somerset House

Sir John Soane's Museum

MUSEUM

 Map p48, H1

This is one of the most fascinating sights in London. Sir John Soane was the architectural genius behind the Bank of England and his former home is now a museum containing all the bits of architectural bric-a-brac that Soane accumulated. The candlelit evenings (first Tuesday of the month) are magical (but queues are long). (www.soane.org; 13 Lincoln's Inn Fields, WC2; admission free; ☺10am-5pm Tue-Sat, 6-9pm 1st Tue of month; ❸Holborn)

Courtauld Gallery

GALLERY

7 ◉ Map p48, H4

The Courtauld Gallery contains a wealth of masterpieces by Rubens, Botticelli, Cézanne, Degas, Renoir, Manet and Monet, to mention but a few, and is particularly known for its Impressionist collection. There are free, 15-minute lunchtime talks on specific works or themes from the collection at 1.15pm every Monday and Friday and on Wednesday during term time. (www.courtauld.ac.uk; Somerset House, The Strand, WC2; adult/child £6/free Tue-Sun, £3/free Mon; ☺10am-6pm; ❸Charing Cross, Embankment, Temple)

Understand
The Fourth Plinth

Three of the four plinths at Trafalgar Sq's corners are occupied by notables but one, originally intended for a statue of William IV, has remained largely vacant for the past 150 years. The Royal Society of Arts conceived the **Fourth Plinth Project** (www.london.gov.uk/fourthplinth) in 1999, for works by contemporary artists. Of three commissioned works, thought-provoking pieces included Rachel Whiteread's *Monument* (2001), a resin copy of the plinth, turned upside down and Anthony Gormley's *One & Other* (2009), presenting the plinth as a space for individuals to occupy.

The Mayor's office has since taken over the Fourth Plinth Project, continuing with the left-field contemporary art theme. Katharina Fritsch's *Hahn/Cock*, a huge, bright blue sculpture of a cockerel, was unveiled in July 2013 and will be exhibited for 18 months.

London Transport Museum
MUSEUM

8 Map p48, G3

One of our favourite 'other' museums, this place looks at how London developed as a result of better transport, and contains everything from horse-drawn omnibuses, early taxis, underground trains you can drive yourself and everything in-between. Check out the museum shop for original and interesting souvenirs, including a great selection of historical tube posters. (www.ltmuseum.co.uk; Covent Garden Piazza, WC2; adult/child £15/free; ⏰10am-6pm Sat-Thu, 11am-6pm Fri; ⊖Covent Garden)

St Martin-in-the-Fields
CHURCH

9 Map p48, F5

The 'royal parish church' is a delightful fusion of classical and baroque styles completed by James Gibbs in 1726. It serves as a model for many churches in New England. Well known for its excellent classical music concerts, many by candlelight, it also has a wonderful cafe in the crypt that hosts jazz evenings once a week. (www.stmartin-in-the-fields.org; Trafalgar Sq, WC2; ⏰8.30am-6pm Mon, Tues, Thu & Fri, 8.30am-5pm Wed, 9.30am-6pm Sat, 3.30-5pm Sun, usually shuts 1hr at lunch; ⊖Charing Cross)

Eating

Dishoom
INDIAN £

10 Map p48, E3

This laid-back eatery takes the fast-disappearing old-style `Bombay cafe' and gives it new life. It's distressed with a modern twist – all ceiling fans and Bollywood photos. Dishes include caff favourites like lamb raan bun, a spicy pulled lamb 'sandwich', okra fries and snack foods such as *bhel poori* (a sweet and sour, soft and crunchy 'party mix' snack). (☎020-7420 9320; www.dishoom.com; 12 Upper St Martin's Lane, WC2; dishes £4-12.50; ⊗8am-11pm Mon-Thu, 8am-midnight Fri, 10am-midnight Sat, 10am-10pm Sun; ⊖Covent Garden)

Nordic Bakery
SCANDINAVIAN £

 11 Map p48, B4

This is the perfect place to escape the chaos that is Soho and relax in the dark-wood-panelled space on the south side of a delightful 'secret' square. Lunch on Scandinavian smoked-fish sandwiches, goat's cheese and beetroot salad or have an after-noon break with tea/coffee and rustic oatmeal cookies. (www.nordicbakery.com; 14a Golden Sq, W1; snacks £4-5; ⊗8am-8pm Mon-Fri, 9am-7pm Sat, 10am-7pm Sun; ⊖Piccadilly Circus)

Brasserie Zédel
FRENCH ££

12 Map p48, C4

This brasserie in the renovated art deco ballroom of a former Piccadilly hotel is the French-est eatery west of Calais. Choose from among the usual favourites, including *choucroute alsacienne* (sauerkraut with sausages and charcuterie, £14) and duck leg confit with Puy lentils. The set menus (£8.25/11.75 for two/three courses) and plats du jour (£12.95) offer excellent value. (☎020-7734 4888; www. brasseriezedel.com; 20 Sherwood St, W1; mains £8-20; ⊗8am-11pm Mon-Fri, noon-11pm Sat, noon-8pm Sun ; ⊖Piccadilly Circus)

Yauatcha
CHINESE ££

13 Map p48, C3

This most glamorous of dim sum restaurants is divided into two: the upstairs dining room offers a delightful blue-bathed oasis of calm from the chaos of Berwick St Market, while downstairs has a smarter, more atmospheric feel, with constellations of 'star' lights. Both serve exquisite dim sum and have a fabulous range of teas. (☎020-7494 8888; www.yauatcha. com; 15 Broadwick St, W1; dishes £4-17; ⊗noon-11.30pm Mon-Sat, to 10.30pm Sun; ⊖Piccadilly Circus, Oxford Circus)

Portrait
MODERN EUROPEAN ££

This stunningly located restaurant above the National Portrait Gallery (see 2 Map p48, E5), with views over Trafalgar Sq and Westminster, is a great place to relax after a morning or afternoon at the gallery; the brunch (10am to 11.30am daily) and afternoon

Local Life
Afternoon Tea

Afternoon tea in the parlour of the **Dean Street Townhouse** (☎020-7434 1775; www.deanstreettownhouse. com; 69-71 Dean St, W1; afternoon tea £16.75; ⊗3-6pm; ⊖Tottenham Court Rd) hardly gets better; it's old-world cosy, with its upholstered furni-ture and roaring fireplace, and the pastries are divine. In summer, you can enjoy eating at one of the few tables on the street terrace.

tea (3.30pm to 4.45pm daily) are recommended. Booking is advisable. Set meals are £25/30 for two/three courses. (☑020-7312 2490; www.npg.org.uk/visit/shop-eat-drink.php; 3rd fl, National Portrait Gallery, St Martin's Pl, WC2; mains £18.50; ☺11.45am-2.45pm daily, 5.30-8.15pm Thu-Sat; ⊖Charing Cross)

Mildreds VEGETARIAN £

14 Map p48, B3

Central London's most inventive vegetarian restaurant, Mildreds heaves at lunchtime so don't be shy about sharing a table in the skylit dining room. Expect the likes of Sri Lankan sweet potato and cashew nut curry, pumpkin and ricotta ravioli, Middle Eastern meze, wonderfully exotic (and filling) salads and delicious stir-fries. There

✓ Top Tip
West End on the Cheap
London, the West End especially, can be an expensive destination but there are plenty of tricks to make your pennies last. Many of the top museums are free, so give them priority over the more commercial attractions. The West End is also compact, so walk, take the bus (cheaper than the tube) or hop on a Barclay's bike. Finally, go out early; most bars in the West End offer happy hour until 8pm or 9pm and, when it's over, head to the pub for a good ol' pint instead of a fancy cocktail.

are also vegan and gluten-free options. (www.mildreds.co.uk; 45 Lexington St, W1; mains £8-10.50; ☺noon-11pm Mon-Sat; ✈; ⊖Oxford Circus, Piccadilly Circus)

Andrew Edmunds MODERN EUROPEAN ££

15 Map p48, B3

This cosy little place, going strong since 1986, is exactly the sort of restaurant you wish you could find everywhere in Soho. Two floors of wood-panelled bohemia with a hand-written menu of French (confit of duck) and European (beetroot and goat's cheese tart) country cooking – it's a real find and reservations are essential. (☑020-7437 5708; www.andrewedmunds.com; 46 Lexington St, W1; mains £11.50-19.50; ☺noon-3.30pm & 5.30-10.45pm Mon-Fri, 12.30-3.30 & 5.30-10.45pm Sat, 1-4pm & 6-10.30pm Sun; ⊖Oxford Circus, Piccadilly Circus)

Great Queen Street BRITISH ££

16 Map p48, G2

The menu at what is one of Covent Garden's best places to eat is seasonal and changes daily, with an emphasis on hearty dishes and good ingredients: think delicious stews, roasts and simple fish dishes. The atmosphere is lively, with a small bar downstairs, and the staff is knowledgeable about the food and wine served. Booking is essential. (☑020-7242 0622; 32 Great Queen St, WC2; mains £12-16; ☺noon-2.30pm & 6-10.30pm Mon-Sat, noon-3pm Sun; ⊖Holborn)

Andrew Edmunds

Bocca di Lupo ITALIAN ££

17  Map p48, C4

Hidden in a dark Soho backstreet, Bocca radiates elegant sophistication. The menu has dishes from across Italy (listing which region they're from) and every main course can be ordered as a small or large portion. There's a good choice of Italian wines and fantastic desserts. It's often full so be sure to book. (☏020-7734 2223; www. boccadilupo.com; 12 Archer St, W1; mains £8-27.50; ☺12.30-3.45pm & 5.30-11pm Mon-Sat, to 9pm Sun; ☻Piccadilly Circus)

Baozi Inn CHINESE £

18 Map p48, E3

Decorated in a vintage style that plays at kitsch communist pop (complete with old Chinese communist military marches tinkling out of the speakers), Baozi Inn serves quality Beijing- and Chengdu-style street food, such as dan dan noodles with spicy pork and baozi buns (steamed buns with stuffing) handmade daily. It's authentic, delicious and cheap food in often-unreliable Chinatown. (25 Newport Ct, WC2; mains £5-7.50; ☺noon-10.30pm Sun-Thu, to 11pm Fri & Sat; ☻Leicester Sq)

Local Life
Fun at Somerset House

The courtyard of Somerset House is transformed into a popular ice rink in winter and used for concerts and events in summer; the **Summer Screen** (when the Great Court turns into an outdoor cinema for 10 evenings in early August) is particularly popular, so book ahead. Behind the house, there's a sunny terrace and cafe overlooking the embankment.

Drinking

Opium   COCKTAIL BAR

19 Map p48, D3

Towering above Chinatown's main drag, what touts itself as a `cocktail and dim sum parlour' could easily pass as an opium den-cum-brothel. Everything is in various shades of scarlet and the bottles have no labels – but rest assured, the cocktails are fantastic and highly unusual. The dim sum menu (£7 to £11) changes daily. Call ahead. (☎020-7734 7276; www.opiumchinatown.com; 15-16 Gerrard St, W1; ⊙5pm-midnight Mon-Wed, to 2am Thu-Sat, noon-midnight Sun)

Lamb & Flag   PUB

20 Map p48, F3

Pocket-sized but packed with charm and history, the Lamb & Flag is still going strong after three and a half centuries (indeed, the poet John Dryden was mugged outside in 1679).

Rain or shine, you'll have to elbow your way to the bar through the merry crowd drinking outside. Inside, it's all brass fittings and creaky wooden floors. (www.lambandflagcoventgarden.co.uk; 33 Rose St, WC2; ⊙11am-11pm Mon-Sat, noon-10.30pm Sun ; ⊖Covent Garden)

LAB Soho   COCKTAIL BAR

21 Map p48, D3

A firm Soho favourite for over a decade, the London Academy of Bartenders (to give it its full name) has some of the best cocktails in town. The list is the size of a small book but, fear not, if you can't make your way through it, just tell the bartenders what you feel like and they'll concoct something suitable. (www.labbaruk.com; 12 Old Compton St, W1; ⊙4pm-midnight Mon-Sat, to 10.30pm Sun; ⊖Leicester Sq, Tottenham Court Rd)

Gordon's Wine Bar   BAR

22 Map p48, G5

A victim of its own success, Gordon's is relentlessly busy and unless you arrive before the office crowd (around 6pm), you can forget about scoring a table. It's cavernous and dark, with French and New World wines both heady and reasonably priced, plus you can nibble on bread, cheese and olives. There's outside garden seating in summer. (www.gordonswinebar.com; 47 Villiers St, WC2; ⊙11am-11pm Mon-Sat, noon-10pm Sun ; ⊖Embankment)

Heaven
GAY

23 📍 Map p48, F5

This long-standing, perennially popular club under the arches beneath Charing Cross station has always played host to good club nights. Monday's Popcorn (mixed dance party, all-welcome door policy) is easily one of the best weeknight clubbing nights in the capital. The celebrated G-A-Y takes place here on Thursday (G-A-Y Porn Idol), Friday (G-A-Y Camp Attack) and Saturday (plain ol' G-A-Y). (www.heavennightclub-london.com; Villiers St, WC2; ⏰11pm-5am Mon, Thu & Fri, 10pm-5am Sat; 🚇Embankment, Charing Cross)

White Horse
PUB

24 📍 Map p48, C3

A lovely pub in a very busy corner of Soho, the White Horse ticks all the boxes: friendly staff, cheap drinks (it's part of the Sam Smith brewery empire) and a great traditional interior with etched glass and wood panels. The upstairs area is particularly cosy and usually quieter than downstairs. (45 Rupert St, W1; ⏰noon-11pm Mon-Sat, to 10.30pm Sun; 🚇Piccadilly Circus, Leicester Sq)

Edge
GAY

25 📍 Map p48, C2

Overlooking Soho Sq in all its four-storey glory, the Edge is London's largest gay bar and heaves every night of the week: there are dancers, waiters in skimpy outfits, good music and a superfriendly vibe, with a heavy straight presence, given its proximity to Oxford St. (www.edgesoho.co.uk; 11 Soho Sq, W1; ⏰3pm-1am Mon-Thu, to 3am Fri & Sat, to 11.30pm Sun; 🚇Tottenham Court Rd)

Candy Bar
LESBIAN

26 📍 Map p48, C2

Also known as Ku Bar Girls, this brilliant watering hole has been the centre of London's small but active lesbian scene for years. Busy most nights of the week, this is very much a girls' space (though one male guest per two women are allowed) and should definitely be your first port of call on the London lesbian scene. (www.ku-bar.co.uk; 4 Carlisle St, W1; ⏰3pm-3am Mon & Wed-Fri, from 1pm Sat, 1-9.30pm Sun; 🚇Tottenham Court Rd)

 Top Tip

An Afternoon at the Opera

Midweek matinees at the Royal Opera House are usually much cheaper than evening performances, with restricted-view seats costing as little as £7. There are same-day tickets (one per customer available to the first 67 people in the queue) from 10am for £8 to £40. Half-price standby tickets are only occasionally available. Otherwise, full-price tickets go for anything up to £120.

Entertainment

Royal Opera House
OPERA

27 Map p48, G3

The £210-million redevelopment for the millennium gave opera a fantastic setting in London and coming here for a night is a sumptuous affair. Although the program has been fluffed up by modern influences, the main attractions are still the opera and classical ballet. (✆020-7304 4000; www.roh.org.uk; Bow St, WC2; tickets £7-175; ⊖Covent Garden)

Comedy Store
COMEDY

28 ⭐ Map p48, D4

This was one of the first comedy clubs in London. Wednesday and Sunday night's Comedy Store Players is the most famous improvisation outfit in town, with Josie Lawrence; on Thurs-

☑️ Top Tip
West End Budget Flicks
Ticket prices at Leicester Sq cinemas are scandalous, so wait for the first-runs to finish and head to the **Prince Charles** (www.princecharlescinema.com; 7 Leicester Pl, WC2; ⊖Leicester Sq), central London's cheapest cinema, where non-members only have to pay £5.50 to £6.50 (or £8 to £10 for new releases). There are also minifestivals, Q&As with film directors, old classics and, most famously, sing-along screenings.

days, Fridays and Saturdays Best in Stand Up features the best of London's comedians. (✆0844 871 7699; www.thecomedystore.co.uk; 1a Oxendon St, SW1; admission £15-22.50; ⊖Piccadilly Circus)

Ronnie Scott's
JAZZ

29 ⭐ Map p48, D3

Ronnie Scott originally opened his jazz club on Gerrard St in 1959 under a Chinese gambling den. The club moved to its current location six years later and became known as Britain's best jazz club. Gigs are at 8.30pm (8pm Sunday) with a second one at 11.15pm Friday and Saturday. Expect to pay between £20 and £50. (✆020-7439 0747; www.ronniescotts.co.uk; 47 Frith St, W1; ⏱6.30pm-3am Mon-Sat, to midnight Sun; ⊖Leicester Sq, Tottenham Court Rd)

Soho Theatre
COMEDY

30 ⭐ Map p48, C2

The Soho Theatre has developed a superb reputation for showcasing new comedy-writing talent. It's also hosted some top-notch stand-up comedians including Alexei Sayle and Doc Brown. Tickets cost between £10 and £20. (✆020-7478 0100; www.sohotheatre.com; 21 Dean St, W1; ⊖Tottenham Court Rd)

Amused Moose Soho
COMEDY

31 ⭐ Map p48, D2

One of the city's best clubs, the Amused Moose (Moonlighting is just one of its host venues) is popular with audiences and comedians alike, perhaps helped along by the fact that

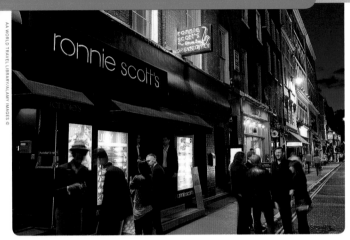

Ronnie Scott's

heckling is 'unacceptable' and all of the acts are 'first-date friendly' (ie unlikely to humiliate the front row). (www.amusedmoose.com; Moonlighting Nightclub, 17 Greek St , W1; ⊖Tottenham Court Rd)

Borderline
CONCERT VENUE

32 ⭐ Map p48, D2

This packed, 275-capacity venue punches above its weight. Crowded House, REM, Blur, Counting Crows, PJ Harvey, Lenny Kravitz, Debbie Harry, plus many anonymous indie outfits, have all played here. The crowd is diverse but full of music journos and record-company A&R types. (www.mamacolive.com/theborderline; Orange Yard, off Manette St, W1; ⊖Tottenham Court Rd)

Curzon Soho
CINEMA

33 ⭐ Map p48, D3

The Curzon Soho is one of London's best cinemas, with a program of the best of British, European, world and American indie films. There are regular Q&As with directors, and mini-festivals, a Konditor & Cook cafe upstairs, cakes to die for and a bar. Tickets are between £8 and £14. (www.curzoncinemas.com; 99 Shaftesbury Ave, W1; ⊖Leicester Sq, Piccadilly Circus)

London Coliseum
OPERA

34 ⭐ Map p48, F4

The Coliseum is home to the English National Opera (ENO), celebrated for making opera modern, as all productions are sung in English. The building, built in 1904 and restored 100 years later, is impressive. The English National Ballet also performs regularly here. Tickets range from £12 to £99. (☑020-7845 9300; www.eno.org; St Martin's Lane, WC2; ⊖Leicester Sq)

Shopping

Stanford's   BOOKS, MAPS

35 🔒 Map p48, F3

As a 150-year-old seller of maps, guides and literature, the grand-daddy of travel bookshops is a destination in its own right. Ernest Shackleton and David Livingstone and, more recently, Michael Palin and Brad Pitt have all popped in. (www.stanfords.co.uk; 12-14 Long Acre, WC2; ⏱9am-8pm Mon-Fri, from 10am Sat, noon-6pm Sun; ⊖Leicester Sq, Covent Garden)

Hamleys   TOYS

36 🔒 Map p48, A3

Said to be the largest toy store in the world, Hamleys is spread over five floors, with computer games next to preschool toys, girls' stuff opposite model cars and science kits next to the latest playground trends. It's topped off with World of Lego and a cafe on the 5th floor. (www.hamleys.com; 188-196 Regent St, W1; ⏱10am-8pm Mon-Fri, 9.30am-8pm Sat, noon-6pm Sun; ⊖Oxford Circus)

Liberty   DEPARTMENT STORE

37 🔒 Map p48, A3

A blend of contemporary styles in a mock-Tudor building, Liberty has a huge cosmetics department and an accessories floor, along with a lingerie section, all at very inflated prices. A classic London souvenir is some Liberty-print fabric, especially in the

---

Understand
Regent Street

- -

Regent St is the curving border dividing Soho's hoi polloi from the high-society residents of Mayfair. Designed by John Nash as a ceremonial route, it was meant to link the Prince Regent's long-demolished city dwelling with the 'wilds' of Regent's Park, and was conceived by the architect as a grand thoroughfare that would be the centrepiece of a new grid for this part of town. Alas, it was never to be – too many toes were being stepped on and Nash had to downscale his plan.

There are some elegant shopfronts that look older than their 1920s origins (when the street was remodelled) but chain stores have almost completely taken over. The street's most famous retail outlet is undoubtedly Hamleys (p60). Regent St is also famous for its Christmas lights displays, which are turned on with great pomp in late November every year.

form of a scarf. (www.liberty.co.uk; Great
Marlborough St, W1; ⊙10am-8pm Mon-Sat,
noon-6pm Sun; ⊖Oxford Circus)

Waterstone's BOOKS

38 Map p48, B5

This is the largest bookshop in
Europe, boasting knowledgeable staff
and author readings. It's spread across
four floors, and there's a rooftop bar-
restaurant, **5th View**. (www.waterstones.
com; 203-206 Piccadilly, W1; ⊙9am-10pm
Mon-Sat, noon-6pm Sun; ⊖Piccadilly Circus)

Agent Provocateur LINGERIE

39 Map p48, C2

Head here for women's lingerie that
is to be worn and seen, not hidden.
Established by Joseph Corre, Vivienne
Westwood's son, its corsets and night-
ies for all shapes and sizes exude confi-
dent sexuality. (www.agentprovocateur.com;
6 Broadwick St, W1; ⊙11am-7pm Mon-Wed, Fri
& Sat, noon-5pm Sun ; ⊖Oxford Circus)

Sister Ray MUSIC

40 Map p48, C2

If you were a fan of the late John Peel
on the BBC/BBC World Service, this
specialist in innovative, experimental
and indie music is your kind of place.
(www.sisterray.co.uk; 34-35 Berwick St,
W1; ⊙10am-8pm Mon-Sat, noon-6pm Sun;
⊖Oxford Circus, Tottenham Court Rd)

Gallery One ART

41 🔒 Map p48, G3

This gallery stocks an excellent and
diverse collection of contemporary art,
both on paper and canvas, framed or
unframed, as well as some cutting-
edge photography. It's all pretty decorative stuff but a world apart from the
usual designer art sold to fill in the
gaps on the wall. (www.g-1.com; 20 Market
Bldg, Covent Garden, WC2; ⊖Covent Garden)

Sting FASHION

42 🔒 Map p48, C4

This Dutch chain is a 'network of
brands' stocking European labels little
known in the UK. Spread over three
floors are anything from casual sweat-
pants and fluoro T-shirts to elegant
dresses and handsome shirts. (www.
thesting.nl; 55 Regent St, W1; ⊙10am-10pm
Mon-Sat, noon-6pm Sun; ⊖Piccadilly Circus)

Vintage House DRINK

43 🔒 Map p48, D3

A whisky connoisseur's paradise,
this shop stocks more than 1400
single-malts, from smooth Macallan
to peaty Lagavulin. It also offers a
huge array of spirits and liqueurs that
you wouldn't find in your average
off-license. (http://freespace.virgin.net/
vintagehouse.co; 42 Old Compton St, W1;
⊙9am-11pm Mon-Fri, 10am-11pm Sat, noon-
10pm Sun; ⊖Leicester Sq)

Explore

British Museum & Bloomsbury

Bookish Bloomsbury puts a leisurely and genteel spin on central London. Home to the British Museum, the British Library, universities, publishing houses, literary pubs and gorgeous Georgian squares, Bloomsbury is deeply but accessibly cultured. You could spend all day in the British Museum, but there's a tantalising choice of options outside, with excellent pubs and restaurants nearby.

The Sights in a Day

☀️ The **British Museum** (p64) is one of London's top sights, so arrive early to do it justice. You will need at least the entire morning here to make any headway, so plan to see the highlights, including the Parthenon Marbles, the Rosetta Stone and the Mummy of Katebet, or split your time between the permanent collection and the temporary exhibitions, which are invariably great.

☀️ Have lunch at **Abeno** (p75) before ambling down to King's Cross. Bibliophiles and library lovers will find the **British Library** (p72) a true eye-opener. Lovers of fine architecture should get on a tour of the exquisite **St Pancras Chambers** (p73) building to admire Victorian design and revel in historical anecdotes.

🌙 Bloomsbury has an alluring selection of international restaurants for dinner, such as **Hakkasan** (p76). Embark on a local pub crawl via the neighbourhood's historic and literary watering holes or drop by **12 Bar Club** (p79) or **Pizza Express Jazz Club** (p79) to see what's on the music menu.

For a local's day in Bloomsbury, see p68.

 Top Sights

British Museum (p64)

 Local Life

A Literary Walk Around Bloomsbury (p68)

💜 **Best of London**

Drinking & Nightlife
Queen's Larder (p69)

London Cocktail Club (p77)

Hidden Sights
Wellcome Collection (p72)

St Pancras Chambers (p73)

Bedford Square (p78)

For Kids
British Museum (p64)

North Sea Fish Restaurant (p76)

Getting There

🚇 **Tube** Take the tube to Tottenham Court Rd (Northern Line or Central Line), Goodge St (Northern Line), Russell Sq (Piccadilly Line) or Euston Sq (Circle, Hammersmith & City and Metropolitan lines).

🚌 **Bus** For the British Museum and Russell Sq, take the handy 24-hour bus 7 along Oxford St; bus 91 runs from Whitehall/Trafalgar Sq to the British Library.

Top Sights
British Museum

The British Museum draws an average of 5.5 million visitors each year. It's an exhilarating stampede through world cultures, with galleries devoted to ancient civilisations, from Egypt to Western Asia, the Middle East, the Romans and Greece, India, Africa, prehistoric and Roman Britain and medieval antiquities. Founded in 1753 following the bequest of royal physician Hans Sloane's 'cabinet of curiosities', the museum expanded its collection through judicious acquisitions and the controversial plundering of empire.

👁 Map p70, C6

📞 020-7323 8000

www.britishmuseum.org

Great Russell St, WC1

admission free

🕙 10am-5.30pm Sat-Thu, to 8.30pm Fri

🚇 Russell Sq, Tottenham Court Rd

Ancient Egypt collection, British Museum

Don't Miss

Great Court

Covered with a spectacular glass-and-steel roof designed by Sir Norman Foster in 2000, the Great Court is the largest covered public square in Europe. In its centre is the world-famous Reading Room, formerly the British Library, which has been frequented by all the big brains of history, from Mahatma Gandhi to Karl Marx.

Ancient Egypt

The star of the show at the British Museum is the Ancient Egypt collection. It comprises sculpture, fine jewellery, papyrus texts, coffins and mummies, including the beautiful and intriguing Mummy of Katebet (room 63). Perhaps the most prized item in the collection is the Rosetta Stone (room 4), the key to deciphering Egyptian hieroglyphics.

Parthenon Sculptures
ROOM 18

Another highlight of the museum is the Parthenon Sculptures (aka Parthenon Marbles). The marble works are thought to show the great procession to the temple that took place during the Panathenaic Festival, on the birthday of Athena, one of the grandest events in the Greek world.

Mosaic Mask of Tezcatlipoca
ROOM 27

Kids will love the Mexican gallery, with the 15th-century Aztec Mosaic Mask of Tezcatlipoca (or Skull of the Smoking Mirror), a human skull decorated with turquoise mosaic. Believed to represent Tezcatlipoca, a creator deity, the skull employs a real human skull as a base for its construction, emblazoned with turquoise, lignite, pyrite and shell.

☑ Top Tips

▶ There are 15 free 30- to 40-minute **Eye-opener tours** of individual galleries throughout the day.

▶ The museum has also developed excellent multimedia **iPad tours** (adult/child £5/3.50). They offer six themed tours each lasting one hour, as well as eight special children's trails lasting 35 minutes each.

▶ **Highlights tours** (adult/child £12/free) depart at 11.30am and 2pm Saturday and Sunday.

▶ A major new extension called the **World Conservation and Exhibitions Centre** was due to open in early 2014 with an exhibition on the Vikings.

✕ Take a Break

The British Museum is vast so you'll need to recharge. Abeno (p75) is nearby for scrumptious savoury pancakes and other dishes from Japan.

China, South Asia & Southeast Asia
ROOM 33

Visit this magnificent gallery, where the impact of Buddhism and other religious beliefs is explored through a stunning collection of objects from China, Tibet, Thailand, Cambodia and other Eastern nations and civilisations. The Qing dynasty gilt bronze mandala is a gorgeous Chinese specimen, with pronounced Tibetan Lamaist motifs.

Roman & Medieval Britain
ROOMS 40 TO 51

Amid all the highlights from ancient Egypt, Greece and Rome, it almost comes as a surprise to see treasures from Britain and nearby Europe (rooms 40 to 51). Many go back to Roman times, when the empire spread across much of the continent, but not all.

Sutton Hoo Ship-Burial
ROOM 41

This elaborate Anglo-Saxon burial site from Suffolk (Eastern England) dates back to the 7th century; items include coins and a stunning helmet complete with face mask.

Lindow Man
ROOM 50

These remains of a 1st-century man were discovered in a bog near Manchester in northern England in 1984. Thanks to the conditions in the bog, many of the internal organs, skin and hair were preserved and scientists were able to determine the nature of Lindow Man's death: an axe stroke to the head and garrotted.

Oxus Treasure
ROOM 52

Dating largely from the 5th to 4th centuries BC, this dazzling collection of around 170 pieces of Achaemenid Persian metalwork was found by the River Oxus, possibly once displayed in a temple. The collection features a host of objects, including model chariots, bracelets, statuettes, vessels and other skilfully fashioned gold and silver pieces.

King's Library

The King's Library is not only a stunning neoclassical space, it also goes back to how we became interested in the history of civilisations, and how disciplines such as biology, archaeology, linguistics and geography all emerged during the 18th century ('the Enlightenment') in a quest for knowledge.

Temporary Exhibitions

The British Museum's exhibitions are among the most popular in London, with many (such as The First Emperor: China's Terracotta Army in 2007 and Life and Death: Pompeii and Herculaneum in 2013) selling out weeks in advance.

British Museum

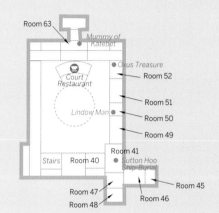

Room 63

Mummy of Katebet

Court Restaurant

Oxus Treasure

Room 52

Room 51

Lindow Man

Room 50

Room 49

Room 41

Stairs Room 40

Sutton Hoo Ship-Burial

Room 45

Room 47

Room 46

Room 48

Upper Floor

China, South Asia & Southeast Asia

Room 33

Court Cafe

Mosaic Mask of Tezcatlipoca

Room 27

Room 4

Great Court Shop

Parthenon Sculptures

Rosetta Stone

Ancient Greece & Rome

Reading Room

King's Library

Ticket Desk (Temporary Exhibitions)

Room 18

Audioguide Desk

Great Court

Stairs

Shop

Gallery Cafe

Ancient Middle East Collection

Cloakroom

Main Entrance

Ground Floor

Great Russell Street

Local Life
A Literary Walk Around Bloomsbury

Bloomsbury is indelibly associated with the literary circles that made this part of London their home. Charles Dickens, JM Barrie, WB Yeats, Virginia Woolf, TS Eliot, Sylvia Plath and other bold-faced names of English literature have all left their names associated with properties delightfully dotted around Bloomsbury and its attractive squares.

❶ Bedford Square

An eye-catching symbiosis of Bloomsbury's creative heritage and architectural charms, Bedford Sq is London's best-preserved Georgian square. The main offices of publishing house Bloomsbury Publishing is at No 50. Sir Anthony Hope Hawkins, author of *The Prisoner of Zenda,* lived at No 41 while the Pre-Raphaelite Brotherhood was founded around the corner at 7 Gower St, 1848.

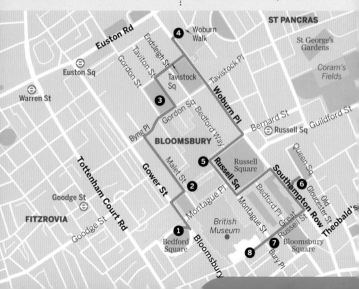

❷ Stroll past Senate House

Along student-thronged Malet St, the splendid but intimidating art deco Senate House served as the Ministry of Information in WWII, providing the inspiration for George Orwell's Ministry of Truth in his dystopian 1948 novel, *Nineteen Eighty-Four*. Orwell's wife, Eileen, worked in the censorship department between 1939 and 1942.

❸ Stop off in Gordon Square

Once a private square, Gordon Sq is open to the public and a lovely place for a rest. Locals sit out on benches reading, chatting and eating sandwiches when the sun shines over Bloomsbury.

❹ WB Yeats & Woburn Walk

Irish poet and playwright WB Yeats lived at 5 Woburn Walk, a genteel lane just south of the church of St Pancras. A leading figure of the Celtic Revival that promoted the native heritage of Ireland and author of *The Tower,* WB Yeats was born in Dublin, but spent many years in London.

❺ Faber & Faber

The former offices of Faber & Faber are at the northwest corner of **Russell Sq**, marked with a plaque to TS Eliot, the American poet and playwright and first editor at Faber. The gardens at the centre of Russell Sq are excellent for recuperation, preferably on a park bench under the trees.

❻ Pop into St George the Martyr

The 18th-century church of **St George the Martyr** (44 Queen Sq) across from the historic **Queen's Larder** (Map p70, D5; www.queenslarder.co.uk; 1 Queen Sq, WC1; ⏱11.30am-11pm Mon-Sat, noon-10.30pm Sun; ⓔRussell Sq) pub at the south end of Queen Sq was where Ted Hughes and Sylvia Plath were married on 16 June 1956 (aka Bloomsday). The couple chose this date to tie the knot in honour of James Joyce.

❼ Literary Shopping

It wouldn't be Bloomsbury without a fine bookshop and the **London Review Bookshop** (www.lrb.co.uk; 14 Bury Pl, WC1; ⏱10am-6.30pm Mon-Sat, noon-6pm Sun; ⓔHolborn) is one of London's finest. Affiliated with literary magazine *London Review of Books*, it features an eclectic selection of books and DVDs; bookworms spend hours browsing the shelves or absorbed in new purchases in the cafe.

❽ Drinks at the Museum Tavern

Karl Marx used to down a well-earned pint at the **Museum Tavern** (www.taylor-walker.co.uk/pub/museum-tavern-bloomsbury/c0747; 49 Great Russell St, WC1; ⏱11am-11.30pm Mon-Thu, to midnight Fri & Sat, 10am-10pm Sun; ⓔHolborn, Tottenham Court Rd) after a hard day inventing communism in the British Museum Reading Room. It's a lovely traditional pub set around a long bar and is popular with academics, students, loyal regulars and tourists alike.

200 m
0.1 miles

HOLBORN

Lincoln's
Inn
Fields

Kingsway

High Holborn

BLOOMSBURY

British
Museum

Russell
Square

Russell Sq

Southampton Row

Theobald's Rd

Bloomsbury Vernon Pl

New Oxford St

Bloomsbury Way

St Giles High St

Charing Cross Rd

Shaftesbury Ave

Tottenham
Court Rd

Tottenham Court Rd

Gower St

Bloomsbury St

New Oxford St

SOHO

Goodge St

Pollock's Toy
Museum

Soho
Square

Sights

Wellcome Collection

MUSEUM

1 Map p70, A4

A 'destination for the incurably curious', this establishment seeks to explore the links between medicine, science, life and art. The heart of the permanent collection is the collection of objects from around the world amassed by pharmacist Sir Henry Wellcome (1853–1936). The museum also runs outstanding exhibitions on topics such as death, drugs, the brain etc. (www.wellcomecollection.org; 183 Euston Rd, NW1; admission free; ☉10am-6pm Tue, Wed, Fri & Sat, 10am-10pm Thu, 11am-6pm Sun; ⊖Euston Sq)

British Library

LIBRARY

2 ◉ Map p70, C2

Amongst the millions of items the British Library keeps, the **Sir John Ritblat Gallery** hosts the most precious. Here you'll find the *Codex Sinaiticus* (the first complete text of the New Testament), Leonardo da Vinci's notebooks, a copy of the *Magna Carta* (1215), explorer Captain Scott's final diary, Shakespeare's First Folio (1623) and original scores by Mozart and Beethoven. (www.bl.uk; 96 Euston Rd, NW1; Ritblat Gallery free; special exhibition cost varies; ☉9.30am-6pm Mon & Wed-Fri, to 8pm Tue, to 5pm Sat, 11am-5pm Sun; ⊙; ⊖King's Cross/St Pancras)

Take a Break Treat yourself to a cup of fine tea and a pastry at Hansom Lounge (p78).

Understand
British Library

In 1998 the British Library moved to its new premises between King's Cross and Euston stations. At a cost of £500 million, it was Britain's most expensive building, and is not universally loved. Colin St John Wilson's exterior of straight lines of red brick, which Prince Charles reckoned was akin to a 'secret-police building', may not be to all tastes, but even those who don't like the building from the outside will be won over by the spectacularly cool and spacious interior.

What you see is just the tip of the iceberg. Under your feet, on five basement levels, run some 625km of shelving (increasing by 12km every year). The library currently contains 180 million items, including 14 million books, 920,000 journal and newspaper titles, 58 million patents, eight million stamps and three million sound recordings.

British Library

St Pancras Chambers

HISTORIC BUILDING

3 Map p70, C2

Looking at the jaw-dropping Gothic elegance of St Pancras, it's hard to believe that the 1873 Midland Grand Hotel languished empty for years and even faced demolition in the 1960s. Now home to a five-star hotel and 66 luxury apartments, St Pancras has been restored to its former glory and can be visited by guided tour (1½ hours, advanced booking only). (☏020-7841 3569; Euston Rd, NW1; £20)

Charles Dickens Museum

MUSEUM

4 Map p70, E4

After a £3.5 million year-long renovation, this museum in a handsome four-storey house – the great Victorian novelist's sole surviving residence in London – is bigger and better than ever. A period kitchen in the basement and a nursery in the attic have been added, and newly acquired 49 Doughty St increases the exhibition space substantially. (www.dickensmuseum.com; 48 Doughty St, WC1; adult/child £8/4; ☉10am-5pm; ☻Chancery Lane, Russell Sq)

Understand

A History of the World in 100 Objects

In 2010, the British Museum launched an outstanding radio series on BBC Radio 4 called *A History of the World in 100 Objects*. The series, presented by British Museum director Neil MacGregor, retraces two million years of history through 100 objects from the museum's collections. Each object is described in a 15-minute program, its relevance and significance analysed. Anyone with access to an MP3 player is encouraged to download the podcasts, available from www.bbc.co.uk/podcasts/series/ahow. Neil MacGregor has also written a book on the topic, *A History of the World in 100 Objects*, published by Penguin.

Pollock's Toy Museum   MUSEUM

5 Map p70, A6

Aimed at adults as much as kids, this museum is simultaneously creepy and mesmerising. You walk in through its shop, laden with excellent wooden toys and various games, and start your exploration by ascending a rickety narrow staircase, where displays begin with mechanical toys, puppets and framed dolls from Latin America, Africa, India and Europe. (www.pollockstoymuseum.com; 1 Scala St, enter from 41 Whitfield St, W1; adult/child £6/3; ⊙10am-5pm Mon-Sat; ⊖Goodge St)

St George's, Bloomsbury   CHURCH

6 Map p70, C7

This superbly restored church designed by Nicholas Hawksmoor (1731) is distinguished by its classical portico of Corinthian capitals and a steeple inspired by the Mausoleum at Halicarnassus and can be seen in William Hogarth's satirical painting *Gin Lane*. The statue at the top is of King George I in Roman dress. (www.stgeorgesbloomsbury.org.uk; Bloomsbury Way, WC1; ⊙9.30am-5.30pm Mon-Fri, 10.30am-12.30pm Sun; ⊖Holborn, Tottenham Court Rd)

Eating

Newman Street Tavern   BRASSERIE ££

7 Map p70, A6

A branch of a prosaic dim sum restaurant chain has metamorphosed into one of the loveliest new brasseries in the West End. As you'll gather from the tray of large crabs and other briny things on display in the front window, the emphasis here is on seafood, with Colchester oysters, Devon crab and local cod in abundance. (☎020-3667 1445; www.newmanstreettavern.co.uk; 48 Newman St, W1; mains £12-20; ⊙noon-11pm Mon-Sat, 10.30am-5pm Sun; ⊖Goodge St)

Peyton & Byrne at the Wellcome Collection
CAFE £

Located in the Wellcome Collection (see 1 ⊙ Map p70, A4), this is a museum cafe like any other, at first sight, with a bright, canteen-like atmosphere, but step closer to the counter and things start looking distinctly gourmet, thanks to freshly made pies and soups, exotic salads and a mouth-watering array of cakes. Everything is top-notch and unbelievably good value. (www.peytonandbyrne.co.uk; Wellcome Collection, 183 Euston Rd, NW1; mains £3-7.50; ⊙10am-6pm Fri-Wed, to 10pm Thu; ⊛; ⊕Euston, Euston Square)

Lady Ottoline
GASTROPUB ££

8 ✗ Map p70, E5

Bloomsbury can feel like a culinary wasteland, but the arrival of this buzzy gastropub named after a patron of the Bloomsbury Set has helped change that. You can eat in the noisy pub downstairs but the cosy dining room above is much nicer. Favourites like Welsh rarebit and steak pies are way better than average. (✆020-7831 0008; www.theladyottoline.com; 11a Northington St, WC1; mains £12-20; ⊙noon-11pm Mon-Sat, to 10.30pm Sun; ⊕Chancery Lane)

Abeno
JAPANESE ££

9 ✗ Map p70

This restaurant specialises in *okonomiyaki*, a Japanese savoury pancake. The pancakes consist of cabbage, egg and flour combined with the ingredients of your choice (there are more than two-dozen varieties, including anything from sliced meats and vegetables to egg, noodles and cheese) and are cooked on your table's hotplate. There are also teppanyaki and yakisoba dishes. (www.abeno.co.uk; 47 Museum St, WC1; mains £9.50-21; ⊙noon-10pm Mon-Sat; ⊕Tottenham Court Rd)

Busaba Eathai
THAI £

10 ✗ Map p70, B6

The Store St premises of this popular mini-chain are slightly less hectic than some of the other West End outlets, but retain all the features that have made it a roaring success: sleek Asian interior, large communal wooden tables and heavenly cheap and tasty Thai dishes like *pad thai,* green and red curries and fragrant noodle soups. (www.busaba.com; 22 Store St, WC1; mains £7-12.50; ⊙noon-11pm Mon-Thu, to 11.30pm Fri & Sat, to 10pm Sun; ⊕Goodge St)

Dabbous
MODERN EUROPEAN ££

11 ✗ Map p70, A6

This award-winning eatery is the creation of Ollie Dabbous, everyone's favourite new chef, so book ahead for dinner or come for lunch (four courses £28). The combination of flavours is inspired – squid with buckwheat, pork with mango, rhubarb with lavender – and at first seems at odds with the industrial decor, but it all works very well. (✆020-7323 1544; www.dabbous.co.uk; 39 Whitfield St, W1; mains £12-16; ⊙noon-3pm & 5.30-11.30pm Tue-Sat; ⊕Goodge St)

North Sea Fish Restaurant

FISH & CHIPS ££

12 Map p70, C3

The North Sea sets out to cook fresh fish and potatoes – a simple ambition in which it succeeds admirably. Look forward to jumbo-sized plaice or halibut fillets, deep-fried or grilled, and huge portions of chips. There's takeaway next door if you can't face the rather austere dining room. (www.northseafishrestaurant.co.uk; 7-8 Leigh St, WC1; mains £10-20; ⊙noon-2.30pm & 5.30-11pm Mon-Sat; ⊖Russell Sq)

Diwana Bhel Poori House

INDIAN £

13 Map p70, A3

Diwana specialises in Bombay-style *bhel poori* (a sweet-and-sour, soft and crunchy 'party mix' snack) and dosas (filled pancakes made from rice flour). You can try thalis (a meal consisting of lots of small dishes, with a focus on vegetables), which offer a selection of tasty treats (£7 to £9) and the

Local Life
Surf & Rest

The British Library has free wi-fi throughout the building. It is therefore a favoured hang-out for students, but visitors can also take advantage of the service while enjoying a break in one of the library's three excellent cafes and restaurants.

all-you-can-eat lunchtime buffet (£7) is legendary. (121-123 Drummond St, NW1; mains £7-9; ⊙noon-11.30pm Mon-Sat, to 10.30pm Sun; ⚲; ⊖Euston, Euston Sq)

Hakkasan

CHINESE £££

14 Map p70, B7

This basement restaurant – hidden down a back alleyway – successfully combines celebrity status, stunning design, persuasive cocktails and sophisticated Chinese food. The low, nightclub-style lighting makes it a good spot for dating or a night out with friends. Book far in advance or come for lunch (three courses for £29, also available from 6pm to 7pm). (☎020-7927 7000; www.hakkasan.com; 8 Hanway Pl, W1; mains £11-61; ⊙noon-12.30am Mon-Wed, to 1.30am Thu-Sat, to midnight Sun; ⊖Tottenham Court Rd)

Drinking

Lamb

PUB

15 Map p70, E5

The Lamb's central mahogany bar with beautiful Victorian dividers (also called 'snob screens' as they allowed the well-to-do to drink in private) has been a favourite with locals since 1729. Nearly three centuries later, its popularity hasn't waned, so come early to bag a booth. There's a decent selection of Young's bitters and a genial atmosphere perfect for unwinding. (www.thelamblondon.com; 94 Lamb's Conduit St, WC1; ⊙noon-11pm Mon-Wed, to midnight Thu-Sat, to 10.30pm Sun; ⊖Russell Sq)

Hakkasan

Queen's Larder
PUB

16 Map p70, D5

In a lovely square southeast of Russell Sq is this pub, so called because Queen Charlotte, wife of 'Mad' King George III, rented part of the pub's cellar to store special foods for her husband while he was being treated nearby. It's a tiny but wonderfully cosy place; there are benches outside for fair-weather fans and a dining room upstairs. (www.queenslarder.co.uk; 1 Queen Sq, WC1; 11.30am-11pm Mon-Sat, noon-10.30pm Sun; Russell Sq)

London Cocktail Club
COCKTAIL BAR

17 Map p70, A6

There are cocktails and then there are cocktails. The guys in this slightly tatty subterranean bar will shake, stir, blend and smoke you some of the most inventive, colourful and punchy concoctions in creation. Try the smoked apple martini or the squid-ink sour. And relax: you'll be staying a lot longer than you thunk (errr, make that thought). (www.londoncocktailclub. co.uk; 61 Goodge St, W1; 4.30pm-midnight Mon-Fri, from 5pm Sat; Goodge St)

Hansom Lounge

CAFE

18 Map p70, C2

Named after the old Hansom cabs (horse-drawn carriages) that once waited in this very place to pick up distinguished guests of the hotel, this elegant cafe occupies the reception area of the Renaissance St Pancras Hotel. The setting is marvellous (brick walls, glass ceilings and those glorious blue steel beams) and the perfect place for tea and pastries. (St Pancras Renaissance London Hotel, Euston Rd, NW1; ⏱7am-10pm; ⊖King's Cross, St Pancras)

Duke

PUB

19 Map p70, E5

As unexpected as sunshine in November, this secluded little pub in the heart of Bloomsbury is a step back in time to the interwar years. Original art deco decor and furnishings are everywhere (burl wood bar, Bakelite phone, pink walls) with Vera Lynn crooning in the background. There are a couple of real ales on offer. (www.dukepub.co.uk; 7 Roger St, WC1; ⏱noon-11pm Mon-Sat, to 10.30pm Sun; ⊖Chancery Lane)

Booking Office

BAR

20 Map p70, C2

As the name suggests, in a former life this was the booking office of St Pancras train station. The space has been transformed into a show-stopping bar, with high ceilings (and prices). The bar has stayed true to its Victorian origins, using plenty of old-fashioned ingredients in its cocktails, such as tea, orange peel, absinthe and gin. (www.bookingofficerestaurant.com; St Pancras Renaissance London Hotel, Euston Rd, NW1; ⏱6.30am-3am; ⊖King's Cross, St Pancras)

Understand

Squares of Bloomsbury

At the very heart of Bloomsbury is **Russell Square**. Originally laid out in 1800 by Humphrey Repton, it was dark and bushy until a striking facelift pruned the trees, tidied up the plants and gave it a 10m-high fountain.

The centre of literary Bloomsbury was **Gordon Square** where, at various times, Bertrand Russell lived at No 57, Lytton Strachey at No 51 and Vanessa and Clive Bell, John Maynard Keynes and the Woolf family at No 46. Strachey, Dora Carrington and Lydia Lopokova (the future wife of Maynard Keynes) all took turns living at No 41. Not all the buildings, many of which now belong to the university, are marked with blue plaques.

Lovely **Bedford Square** is the only completely Georgian square still surviving in Bloomsbury.

Newman Arms
PUB

21 🚇 Map p70, A7

A lovely local that is one of the few family-run pubs in central London, this is a one-room affair with a 150-year history of providing great beer to locals. George Orwell and Dylan Thomas were regulars, and Michael Powell's *Peeping Tom* was filmed here in 1960. There's also an excellent pie (from £10) room upstairs. (www.newmanarms.co.uk; 23 Rathbone St, W1; ⏰noon-11.30pm Mon-Fri; 🚇Goodge St)

Bradley's Spanish Bar
BAR

22 🚇 Map p70, B7

Bradley's is only vaguely Spanish in decor, but much more authentic in its choice of booze: San Miguel, Cruzcampo, *tinto de verano* (red wine with rum and lemonade) and that teen favourite sangria. Punters are squeezed under low ceilings in the nooks of the basement, while a vintage vinyl jukebox plays rock tunes of their choice. (www.bradleysspanishbar.co.uk; 42-44 Hanway St, W1; ⏰noon-11pm Mon-Sat, 3-10.30pm Sun; 🚇Tottenham Court Rd)

Entertainment

12 Bar Club
LIVE MUSIC

23 ⭐ Map p70, B8

Small, intimate and with a rough-and-ready feel, the 12 Bar is a favourite live-music venue, with solo acts and/or bands performing nightly. The emphasis is on songwriting and the music is very much indie rock, with anything from folk and jazzy influences to full-on punk and metal sounds in-between. (www.12barclub.com; Denmark St, WC2; admission £6-10; ⏰7pm-3am Mon-Sat, to 12.30am Sun; 🚇Tottenham Court Rd)

Place
DANCE

24 ⭐ Map p70, B3

One of London's most exciting cultural venues, this was the birthplace of modern British dance and still concentrates on challenging, experimental choreography. Behind the late-Victorian facade there's a 300-seat theatre, an arty, creative cafe atmosphere and a dozen training studios. The Place sponsors an annual Place Prize, which recognises new and outstanding dance talent. Tickets range from £12 to £25. (www.theplace.org.uk; 17 Duke's Rd, WC1; 🚇Euston Sq)

Pizza Express Jazz Club
JAZZ

25 ⭐ Map p70, B8

Believe it or not, Pizza Express is one of the best jazz venues in London. It's a strange arrangement, in a basement beneath the main chain restaurant, but it seems to work. Lots of big names perform here and then-promising artists such as Norah Jones, Jamie Cullum and the late Amy Winehouse played here in their early days. (📞0845 602 7017; www.pizzaexpress-live.com; 10 Dean St, W1; admission £15-20; 🚇Tottenham Court Rd)

Understand
King's Cross Regeneration

King's Cross used to be something of a blind spot on London's map, somewhere you only ever went through rather than to. The area was the capital's red-light district, and when the British Library first opened here in 1998, drug addicts could regularly be found in the toilets.

Fast-forward a decade or two, and King's Cross's transformation is astounding. The two stations, King's Cross and St Pancras, have played a leading role in this rejuvenation: St Pancras first, with the arrival of the Eurostar in 2007 and the opening of the Renaissance St Pancras Hotel in 2011.

Ugly duckling King's Cross is now turning into a swan, with a new departures concourse sitting under a magnificent, canopy-like curving roof, and the double-arched brick facade being given pride of place on the forecourt. Meanwhile, the back of the station is being transformed into desirable real estate. In early 2013, Google announced it would be moving its UK headquarters there in 2016, for the tidy sum of £1 billion.

100 Club
LIVE MUSIC

26 ⭐ Map p70, A7

This legendary London venue has always concentrated on jazz, but it's also spreading its wings to swing and rock. It once showcased Chris Barber, BB King and the Stones, and was at the centre of the punk revolution and the '90s indie scene. It hosts dancing swing gigs and local jazz musicians, as well as the occasional big name. (☎020-7636 0933; www.the100club.co.uk; 100 Oxford St, W1; admission £8-15; ⊖Oxford Circus, Tottenham Court Rd)

Shopping

Bang Bang Clothing Exchange
VINTAGE

27 🔒 Map p70, A6

Bang Bang exchanges, buys and sells designer, high-street and vintage clothing. As they say, 'think of Alexander McQueen cocktail dresses rubbing shoulders with Topshop shoes and 1950s jewellery'. Indeed. (www.bangbangclothingexchange.co.uk; 21 Goodge St, W1; ⊙10am-6.30pm Mon-Fri, 11am-6pm Sat; ⊖Goodge St)

Harry Potter Shop
CHILDREN

28 🔒 Map p70, C2

Harry Potter fans unite; this is your very own window into the world of the child wizard. Set up as a wand shop (wands from around £25), with wood panels and plenty of shelves and drawers, it also sells jumpers sporting the colours of Hogwarts' four houses (Gryffindor having pride of place) and assorted merchandise. (departure concourse, King's Cross station, N1; ⊙10am-6pm; ⊖King's Cross/St Pancras)

James Smith & Sons   ACCESSORIES

 29 Map p70, C7

'Outside every silver lining is a big black cloud', claim the cheerful owners of this quintessential English shop. Nobody makes and stocks such elegant umbrellas, walking sticks and canes as this traditional place does. They've been here since 1857 and, thanks to London's notoriously bad weather, they'll hopefully do great business for years to come. (www.james-smith.co.uk; 53 New Oxford St, WC1; ⊙10am-6pm Mon-Fri, to 5.30pm Sat; ⊖Tottenham Court Rd)

Gay's the Word   BOOKS

30 Map p70, C4

This London gay institution has been selling books nobody else stocks for 35 years and still has a great range of gay- and lesbian-interest books and magazines, as well as a real community spirit. Used books available as well. (www.gaystheword.co.uk; 66 Marchmont St, WC1; ⊙10am-6.30pm Mon-Sat, 2-6pm Sun; ⊖Russell Sq)

Queen's Larder (p77)

Skoob Books   BOOKS

31 Map p70, C4

Skoob (you work out the name) has got to be London's largest secondhand bookshop, with some 60,000 titles spread over 2500 sq ft of floor space. (www.skoob.com; 66 The Brunswick, off Marchmont St, WC1; ⊙10.30am-8pm Mon-Sat, to 6pm Sun ; ⊖Russell Sq)

On the Beat   MUSIC

32 Map p70, B7

Mostly '60s and '70s retro – along with helpful staff – in a tiny room plastered with posters. (22 Hanway St, W1; ⊙11am-7pm; ⊖Tottenham Court Rd)

NEIL SETCHFIELD/GETTY IMAGES ©

Explore

St Paul's & the City

For its size, the City punches well above its weight for attractions, with an embarrassment of sightseeing riches. The heavyweights – the Tower of London and St Paul's – are a must, but combine the other top sights with exploration of the City's lesser-known delights and quieter corners; the scores of churches make peaceful stops along the way.

The Sights in a Day

☀ Make it an early start to get ahead of the crowds besieging the **Tower of London** (p84). Explore **Tower Bridge** (p94) (check the website the day before to see if the bridge is due to be raised) and have a table booked for lunch at **Wine Library** (p99).

☼ Stop at **All Hallows by the Tower** (p94) before heading to **St Paul's Cathedral** (p88), past **Monument** (p94). Take a tour of the cathedral and make your way to the top of the staggering dome for choice views. If you've any time spare, peruse the **Museum of London** (p94).

☾ To wind down, head for cocktails with views at **Madison** (p100) or **Vertigo 42** (p100). Come back down to earth for dinner at **St John** (p99) or **Bread Street Kitchen** (p96) and round up the night in one of the City's historic pubs (note that some may shut at weekends). Shoreditch (p102) also makes a fine alternative for an entertaining and memorable evening out in London.

⊙ Top Sights

St Paul's Cathedral (p88)

Tower of London (p84)

♥ Best of London

Drinking & Nightlife
Folly (p99)

Fabric (p100)

Blackfriar (p100)

Architecture
30 St Mary Axe (p94)

All Hallows by the Tower (p94)

Views
Duck & Waffle (p96)

Monument (p94)

Vertigo 42 (p100)

Getting There

⊖ **Tube** Handiest stations are St Paul's (Central Line) and Bank (Central, Northern and Waterloo & City Lines, and DLR); Blackfriars (Circle and District Lines), Farringdon (Circle, Metropolitan and Hammersmith & City Lines) and Tower Hill (Circle and District Lines) are also useful.

🚍 **Bus** Useful routes include 8, 15, 11 and 26.

Top Sights
Tower of London

The absolute kernel of London, with a history as bleak and bloody as it is fascinating, the Tower of London is one of London's superlative sights. Begun during the reign of William the Conqueror (1066–87), the Tower is actually a castle, and has served through history as a palace, observatory, storehouse and mint. But it is, of course, most famous for its grizzly past as a prison and site of execution. Despite ever-inflating ticket prices and crowds, it remains a must-see.

👁 Map p92, H5

📞 0844 482 7777

www.hrp.org.uk/towerof london

Tower Hill, EC3

adult/child £21.45/10.75

🕙 9am-5.30pm Tue-Sat, from 10am Sun & Mon, to 4.30pm Nov-Feb

🚇 Tower Hill

Tower of London

Don't Miss

Crown Jewels

Waterloo Barracks is home to the magnificent
Crown Jewels. A travelator conveys you past the
dozen crowns that are the centrepiece, including
the £27.5-million Imperial State Crown – set with
diamonds (precisely 2868 of them), sapphires,
emeralds, rubies and pearls – and the platinum
crown of the late Queen Mother, Elizabeth,
famously set with the 105-carat Koh-i-Noor
(Mountain of Light) diamond.

White Tower

Begun in 1078, this was the original 'Tower' of
London, built as a palace and fortress. By modern
standards it's not tall, but in the Middle Ages it
would have dwarfed the surrounding huts of the
peasantry. Inside, along with St John's Chapel,
the tower has retained a couple of remnants of
Norman architecture, including a fireplace and
garderobe (lavatory).

Royal Armouries

Housed within the White Tower, this fabulous
collection of cannons, guns and suits of armour
for men and horses includes Henry VIII's suit
of armour, made when the monarch was in his
forties, the 2m suit of armour made for John
of Gaunt and, alongside it, a tiny child's suit of
armour designed for James I's young son, Henry.

Tower Green Scaffold Site

Anne Boleyn, Catherine Howard, Margaret Pole
(Countess of Salisbury) and 16-year-old Lady
Jane Grey were among the privileged individuals executed here. The site is commemorated
by a sculpture from artist Brian Catling, and a
remembrance poem. To the left of the scaffold
site is the Beauchamp Tower, where high-ranking

☑ Top Tips

▶ Tag along with one of
the Yeoman Warder's
tours.

▶ Avoid immense
queues and arrive as
early as you can to see
the Crown Jewels.

▶ Book online for
cheaper tickets; tickets
bought in advance are
valid for seven days from
the selected date.

▶ If you've a question,
put it to one of the Yeo-
man Warders, who are
happy to help.

✗ Take a Break

The red-brick **New
Armouries Cafe**
(⏱10.30am-5pm Sun &
Mon, from 9.30am Tue-Sat),
in the southeastern cor-
ner of the inner court-
yard offers hot meals
and sandwiches.

Fortify yourself with
wine and eats at nearby
Wine Library (p99), but
book ahead if lunching.

prisoners have left behind melancholic inscriptions.

Chapel Royal of St Peter ad Vincula

The Chapel Royal of St Peter ad Vincula (St Peter in Chains) is a rare example of ecclesiastical Tudor architecture and the burial place of those beheaded on the scaffold outside, most notably Anne Boleyn, Catherine Howard and Lady Jane Grey. Inside (accessible only via tour) are monuments to luminaries from the Tower's history.

Bloody Tower

The Bloody Tower takes its nickname from the 'princes in the tower', Edward V and his younger brother, held here and later murdered. Their uncle Richard III usually takes the blame, but you can vote for your prime suspect at an exhibition here. There are also exhibits on Elizabethan adventurer Sir Walter Raleigh, imprisoned here three times by Elizabeth I.

Medieval Palace

Inside St Thomas' Tower, discover what the hall and bedchamber of Edward I might once have looked like. Opposite St Thomas' Tower is Wakefield Tower, built by Henry III between 1220 and 1240 and now enticingly furnished with a replica throne and candelabra to give an impression of how it might have looked in Edward I's day.

Bowyer Tower

Behind the Waterloo Barracks is the Bowyer Tower, where George, Duke of Clarence, brother and rival of Edward IV, was imprisoned and, according to a long-standing legend that has never been proved, was drowned in a barrel of malmsey (sweet Madeira wine).

East Wall Walk

The huge inner wall of the Tower was added to the fortress in 1220 by Henry III. It takes in Salt Tower, Broad Arrow and Constable Towers and ends with Martin Tower, housing an exhibition of original coronation regalia. Colonel Thomas Blood, disguised as a clergyman, attempted to steal the Crown Jewels from Martin Tower in 1671.

Bell Tower

Housing the curfew bells, the Bell Tower was a one-time lock-up holding Thomas More. The politician and author of *Utopia* was imprisoned here in 1534, before his execution for refusing to recognise King Henry VIII as head of the Church of England in place of the Pope.

Tours

While Yeoman Warders officially guard the tower and Crown Jewels at night, their main role is as tour guides (and to pose for photographs with curious foreigners). These tours, which are often extremely amusing and always informative, leave from the Middle Tower every 30 minutes from 10am to 3.30pm (2.30pm in winter).

Understand
Tower of London

- -

Yeoman Warders
Yeoman Warders have been guarding the tower since the late 15th century. There can be up to 40 (at present there are 37) and, in order to qualify for the job, they must have served a minimum of 22 years in any branch of the British Armed Forces. They live within the tower walls and are known affectionately as 'Beefeaters', a nickname they dislike. The origin of the name is unknown, although it's thought to be due to the large rations of beef – then a luxury food – they were once given. There is currently just one female Yeoman Warder, Moira Cameron, who in 2007 became the first ever woman in the post.

The Ravens
Legend has it that Charles II requested that ravens be kept at the Tower as the kingdom would fall apart if they left. There are usually at least six ravens at the Tower and their wings are clipped to placate the superstitious.

Ceremonies at the Tower
The elaborate locking of the main gates has been performed daily without fail for over 700 years. The ceremony begins at 9.53pm precisely, and it's all over by 10pm. Even when a bomb hit the Tower of London during the Blitz, the ceremony was only delayed by 30 minutes. Entry to the ceremony begins at 9.30pm and is free but, in a suitably antiquated process, you have to apply for tickets by post, as demand is so high. See the Tower website for details.

More accessible is the official unlocking of the Tower, which takes place every day at 9am. The keys are escorted by a military guard and the doors are unlocked by a Yeoman Warder. With fewer visitors around, this is a great time to arrive, although you'll have to wait until 10am on a Sunday or Monday to get in.

Koh-i-Noor Diamond
Surrounded by myth and legend, the 14th-century Koh-i-Noor diamond has been claimed by both India and Afghanistan. It reputedly confers enormous power on its owner, although male owners are destined for a tormented death.

Top Sights
St Paul's Cathedral

Towering over Ludgate Hill, in a superb position that has been a place of worship for over 1400 years, St Paul's Cathedral is one of London's most majestic structures. For Londoners, the vast dome, which still manages to dominate the skyline despite the far higher skyscrapers of the Square Mile, is a symbol of resilience and pride, standing tall for over 300 years. Viewing Sir Christopher Wren's masterwork from the inside, and climbing its height for sweeping views, is exhilarating.

◉ Map p92, C3

www.stpauls.co.uk

St Paul's Churchyard, EC4

adult/child £16/7

🕙 8.30am-4.30pm Mon-Sat, last entry 4pm

🚇 St Paul's

Dome, St Paul's Cathedral

Don't Miss

Dome

London's largest church dome – the structure actually consists of three domes, one inside the other – made the cathedral Wren's tour de force. Exactly 528 stairs take you to the top, but it's a three-stage journey. Through a door on the western side of the southern transept, then some 30m and precisely 257 steps above, you reach the interior walkway around the dome's base.

Whispering Gallery & Stone Gallery

The Whispering Gallery is the first level of your ascent towards the dome. It is so called because if you talk close to the wall it carries your words around to the opposite side, 32m away. Climbing another 119 steps brings you to the Stone Gallery, an exterior viewing platform obscured by pillars and other safety measures.

Golden Gallery

The remaining 152 iron steps to the Golden Gallery are steeper and narrower than the steps below but climbing them is really worth the effort. From here, 85m above London, you can enjoy superb 360-degree views of the city.

Epitaph & Duke of Wellington Memorial

Just beneath the dome is a compass and epitaph written for Wren by his son: *Lector, si monumentum requiris, circumspice* (Reader, if you seek his monument, look around you). In the northern aisle you'll find the grandiose Duke of Wellington Memorial (1912), which took 54 years to complete.

The Light of the World

In the north transept chapel is Pre-Raphaelite artist Holman Hunt's iconic painting, *The Light*

☑ Top Tips

▶ Join a free tour.

▶ Or pick up one of the free 45-minute iPod tours (in multiple languages).

▶ Anyone can use the facilities in the crypt for free, entering via the side door under the north transept. Without a ticket, you can enter the cafe, restaurant and shop, use the toilet or shelter from bad weather.

▶ Enquire at the desk about introductory talks.

▶ Groups of five should consider the one-hour Triforium tour.

✕ Take a Break

The **Restaurant at St Paul's** (☑ 020-7248 2469; www.restaurantatstpauls. co.uk; Crypt, St Paul's Cathedral, EC4; 2-/3-course lunch £21.50/25.95; ⊙ noon-5pm; 🛜; ⊖ St Paul's) offers good-value lunches.

The **Crypt Café** (dishes £5.65-8.25; ⊙ 9am-5pm Mon-Sat, noon-4pm Sun) is handy for light meals.

of the World, which depicts Christ knocking at an overgrown door that, symbolically, can only be opened from the inside.

Quire

Progressing east into the cathedral's heart is the spectacular quire (or chancel) – its ceilings and arches dazzling with green, blue, red and gold mosaics – and the high altar. The ornately carved choir stalls by Grinling Gibbons on either side of the quire are exquisite, as are the ornamental wrought-iron gates, separating the aisles from the altar, by Jean Tijou.

American Memorial Chapel

Walk around the altar, with its massive gilded oak canopy, to the American Memorial Chapel, a memorial to the 28,000 Americans based in Britain who lost their lives during WWII.

Crypt

On the eastern side of the north and south transepts, stairs lead down to the crypt and OBE Chapel where services are held for members of the Order of the British Empire. There are memorials to Florence Nightingale, Lord Kitchener and others; the Duke of Wellington, Christopher Wren and Admiral Nelson are buried here, the latter in a black sarcophagus.

St Paul's Cathedral

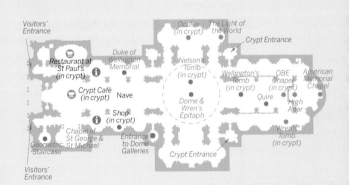

Oculus

The Oculus, opened in 2010 in the former treasury, projects four short films onto its walls. (You'll need to have picked up the iPod audiotour to hear the sound.) If you're not keen on scaling the dome, you can experience it here, audiovisually, from the ground.

Monument to the People of London

Just outside the north transept, there's a simple monument to the people of London, honouring the 32,000 civilians killed (and another 50,000 seriously injured) in the city during WWII.

Temple Bar

To the left as you face the entrance stairway is Temple Bar, one of the original gateways to the City of London. This medieval stone archway once straddled Fleet St at a site marked by a griffin but was removed to Middlesex in 1878. Temple Bar was restored and made a triumphal return to London alongside the redevelopment of Paternoster Sq in 2003.

FEARGUS COONEY/GETTY IMAGES ©

St Paul's Cathedral

Tours

Joining a tour is one of the best ways to explore the cathedral and allows access to the Geometric Staircase and Chapel of St Michael and St George. Tours are usually held six times a day.

HOLBORN

Hatton Garden
Kirby St
Greville St

Farringdon ⊖
Cowcross St
St John St
✕ 18
22 ⊙

⊖ Barbican   Beech St

Silk

✿ 27

Charterhouse St

Smithfield
Market

Long La

Fore St

Little Britain

Museum of
London

16 ✕
⊙ 1

London Wa

Snow Hill
Hosier La
Cock La

West Smithfield

Holborn
Viaduct

Noble St
Wood St

Gresham St

**Angel
St**

Aldersgate

Foster La

29 🔒

15
✕ **New
Fetter La**

St Andrew St

Farringdon St

Shoe La

Bride St

Limeburner La

Newgate St

Central
Criminal
Court

St Paul's ⊖

St Paul's Churchyard

Wood St

Cheapside

King St

26 🍷

Fleet St

Shoe La
Bouverie St

Whitefriars St
Salisbury Ct

Ludgate Hill
🔒 City
Thameslink

Carter La

New Bridge St

St Paul's Churchyard

⊙ **St Paul's
Cathedral**

St Paul's Churchyard

Bread St

25 🔒
⊙ 12 ✕ 14 ✕
Watling St
Bow La

Cannon St

✕ 1

Tudor St

Temple Ave

23 ⊙

Blackfriars ⊖
🚇

**Puddle
Dock**

Queen Victoria St

White Lion Hill

⊖
**Mansion
House**

Upper Thames St

Queen St

Victoria Embankment

Blackfriars
Bridge

Millennium
Bridge

Southw
Bridge

Bankside

Park St

For reviews see

⊙	Top Sights	p84
⊙	Sights	p94
✕	Eating	p96
🍷	Drinking	p99
✿	Entertainment	p101
🔒	Shopping	p101

Ⓝ 0   400 m
    0   0.2 miles

E
F
G
H

Exchange Square

Spitalfields Market 28
Commercial St

Ropemaker St
South Pl
Wilson St
Sun St
Brushfield St
White's Row
BruneSt
1

Moorgate
Eldon St
Liverpool St
Artillery La
Middlesex St
Wentworth St

Moorgate
Finsbury Circus
Blomfield St
Liverpool St
Bishopsgate
New St
Petticoat Lane Market
Goulston St
2

London Wall

Wormwood St
Houndsditch 11
Camomile St
St Mary Axe
Bevis Marks
Bury St
Duke's Pl
Aldgate
Aldgate High St

Coleman St
Moorgate
Throgmorton Ave
Old Broad St 21
Bishopsgate
5
30 St Mary Axe
Mitre St
Creechurch La

Bank of England Museum
Threadneedle St
Leadenhall St
Fenchurch St
Jewry St
Vine St
Minories
3

CITY
9
Princes St
19
Cornhill
24
8
Lloyd's of London
Billiter St
Mark La
America Sq

Ultry
St Stephen Walbrook
Bank
Birchin La
Lime St
Fenchurch St
Crutched Friars

10
King William St
Lombard St
Gracechurch St
Rood La
Roman Wall
Pepys St
17
Roman Wall

Walbrook
Cannon St
20
Eastcheap
Mincing La
St Olave's
Trinity Square
7
Tower Hill
Tower of London
4

Cannon St
Arthur St
3
Monument
Monument St
Great Tower St
6
Tower Hill

Angel Pass
L Pountney La
King William St
Lower Thames St
Byward St
All Hallows by the Tower
4

Old Billingsgate Market
Lower Thames St

River Thames
London Bridge
Tower of London

The Queen's Walk
Tooley St
Tower Bridge 2
5

Sights

Museum of London   MUSEUM

1 ◉ Map p92, C2

One of the capital's best museums, this is a fascinating walk through the various incarnations of the city from Anglo-Saxon village to 21st-century metropolis, contained in two dozen galleries. There are a lot of interactive displays with an emphasis on experience rather than learning. (www.museumoflondon.org.uk; 150 London Wall, EC2; admission free; ◷10am-6pm; ⊖Barbican)

Tower Bridge   BRIDGE

2 ◉ Map p92, H5

London was a thriving port in 1894 when elegant Tower Bridge was built. It was designed to be raised to allow ships to pass, though electricity has now taken over from the original steam and hydraulic engines. A lift leads up the northern tower to the **Tower Bridge Exhibition** (www.towerbridge.org.uk; adult/child £8/3.40; ◷10am-6pm Apr-Sep, 9.30am-5.30pm Oct-Mar; ⊖Tower Hill) in the upper walkway, where the story of the bridge's building is recounted. (⊖Tower Hill)

Monument   TOWER

3 ◉ Map p92, F4

Sir Christopher Wren's 1677 column, known simply as the Monument, is a memorial to the Great Fire of London of 1666, whose impact on London's history cannot be overstated. An immense Doric column made of Portland stone, the Monument is 4.5m wide, and 60.6m tall – the exact distance it stands from the bakery in Pudding Lane where the fire started. (www.themonument.info; Fish Street Hill, EC3; adult/child £3/1; ◷9.30am-5.30pm; ⊖Monument)

All Hallows by the Tower   CHURCH

4 ◉ Map p92, G4

A church by this name (meaning 'all saints') has stood here since AD 675. Despite its proximity to the spot where the Great Fire started (Samuel Pepys watched the blaze from the brick tower), All Hallows survived virtually unscathed, only to be hit by German bombs in 1940. (www.ahbtt.org.uk; Byward St, EC3; admission free; ◷8am-6pm Mon-Fri, 10am-5pm Sat, 10am-1pm Sun; ⊖Tower Hill)

30 St Mary Axe   NOTABLE BUILDING

5 ◉ Map p92, G3

Built in 2002–03 and known to one and all as 'the Gherkin', 30 St Mary Axe remains London's most distinctive skyscraper, dominating the city despite being slightly smaller than the neighbouring NatWest Tower. Sir Norman Foster's phallic sci-fi exterior has become an emblem of modern London, as recognisable as Big Ben or the London Eye. (Gherkin; www.30stmaryaxe.co.uk; 30 St Mary Axe, EC3; ⊖Aldgate)

Trinity Square Gardens   GARDENS

6 ◉ Map p92, H4

Just west of Tower Hill tube station, these gardens were once the site of the Tower Hill scaffold where many

Tower Bridge

met their fate, the last in 1747. Now it's a much more peaceful place, ringed with important buildings and bits of the Roman wall. (◉Tower Hill)

St Olave's
CHURCH

7 ◉ Map p92, G4

Tucked at the end of quiet Seething Lane, St Olave's was built in the mid-15th century and survived the Great Fire. It was bombed in 1941 and restored in the 1950s. The diarist Samuel Pepys worshipped and is buried here; see the tablet on the south wall. Dickens called the place 'St Ghastly Grim' because of the skulls above its entrance. (www.sanctuaryinthecity.net; 8 Hart St, EC3; admission free; ⊘9am-5pm Mon-Fri Sep-Jul; ◉Tower Hill)

Lloyd's of London
NOTABLE BUILDING

8 ◉ Map p92, G3

While the world's leading insurance brokers are inside underwriting everything from cosmonauts' lives to film stars' legs, people outside still stop to gawp at the stainless-steel external ducting and staircases of this 1986 building. Designed by Richard Rogers, one of the architects of the Pompidou Centre in Paris, its brave-new-world postmodernism strikes a particular contrast with the olde-worlde Leadenhall Market next door. (www.lloyds.com/lloyds/about-us/the-lloyds-building; 1 Lime St, EC3; ◉Aldgate, Monument)

Bank of England Museum
MUSEUM

9 Map p92, E3

The centrepiece of this museum, which explores the evolution of money and the history of the venerable Bank of England (founded in 1694), is a reconstruction of the original Bank Stock Office, complete with mahogany counters. The museum is packed with exhibits ranging from silverware and coins to a 13kg gold bar you can lift. (www.bankofengland.co.uk/museum; Bartholomew Lane, EC2; admission free; ⏰10am-5pm Mon-Fri; ⊖Bank)

St Stephen Walbrook
CHURCH

10 Map p92, E3

Just south of Mansion House, St Stephen Walbrook (1672) is considered

---

> **Local Life**
> ## Tale of Two Cities
> While about 300,000 people work in the City of London, only 8000 actually live here. To really appreciate its frantic industry and hum, you're best to come during the week, which is when you'll find everything open. It empties quickly in the evening, as its workers retreat to the suburbs. Weekends have a very different appeal, giving you a lot more space for quiet contemplation – you'll find most places shut tight until Monday though all of the big-hitting sights open on at least one weekend day.

---

to be the finest of Wren's City churches and, as it was his first experiment with a dome, a forerunner to St Paul's Cathedral. Some 16 pillars with Corinthian capitals rise to support the dome; the modern travertine marble altar nicknamed 'the Camembert' is by sculptor Henry Moore. (www.ststephenwalbrook.net; 39 Walbrook, EC4; admission free; ⏰10am-4pm Mon-Fri; ⊖Bank)

Eating

Duck & Waffle
BRASSERIE ££

11 ✕ Map p92, G2

If you like your views with sustenance round the clock, this is the place for you. Perched atop Heron Tower just down from Liverpool St station, its hearty British dishes (lots of offal, some unusual seafood concoctions like pollack meatballs and chip-shop cod tongues) come in small and large sizes by day, waffles by night and drinks any time. (☑020-3640 7310; www.duckandwaffle.com; 40th fl, Heron Tower, 110 Bishopsgate, EC2; mains £7-32; ⏰24hr; ⊖Liverpool St)

Bread Street Kitchen
BRASSERIE ££

12 ✕ Map p92, D3

Gordon Ramsay's latest foray into the City makes us wonder whether he thinks he's actually in East London. The huge warehouse-like space in One New Change contains a raw bar, wine balcony and open kitchen that produces mostly Modern British favourites like mutton and potato pie

Understand
Churches of the City

As befits the oldest part of London, the City has plenty of historic churches where you can explore some of the oldest architecture in town. Some of the most significant:

▶ **All Hallows by the Tower** (p94)

▶ **St Olave's** (p95)

▶ **St Stephen Walbrook** (p96)

▶ **St Mary-le-Bow** (☏020-7248 5139; www.stmarylebow.co.uk; Cheapside, EC2; admission free; ⏱7.30am-6pm Mon-Wed, to 6.30pm Thu, to 4pm Fri; ⊖St Paul's, Bank)

▶ **St Lawrence Jewry** (www.stlawrencejewry.org.uk; Gresham St, EC2; admission free; ⏱8am-4pm; ⊖Bank)

▶ **St Bartholomew-the-Great** (www.greatstbarts.com; West Smithfield, EC1; adult/ concession £4/3.50; ⏱8.30am-5pm Mon-Fri, 10.30am-4pm Sat, 8.30am-8pm Sun; ⊖Farringdon or Barbican)

▶ **St Bride's, Fleet Street** (☏020-7427 0133; www.stbrides.com; Bride Lane, EC4; donation requested £2; ⏱8am-6pm Mon-Fri, hrs vary Sat, 10am-6.30pm Sun; ⊖St Paul's, Blackfriars)

and roasted cod. 'Lazy Loaf' brunch just might lure the crowds to the City on a Sunday. (☏020-3030 4050; www. breadstreetkitchen.com; 10 Bread St, EC4; mains £12-19; ⏱7am-midnight Mon-Fri, from noon Sat & Sun; ⊖St Paul's)

Sweeting's SEAFOOD £££

 13 Map p92, D3

Sweeting's is a City institution, having been around since 1889. It hasn't changed much, with its small sit-down dining area, mosaic floor and narrow counters, behind which stand wait-

ers in white aprons. Dishes include sustainably sourced fish of all kinds (grilled, fried or poached), potted shrimps, eels and Sweeting's famous fish pie (£13.50). (☏020-7248 3062; www. sweetingsrestaurant.com; 39 Queen Victoria St, EC4; mains £13.50-35; ⏱11.30am-3pm Mon-Fri; ⊖Mansion House)

Café Below CAFE £

 14 Map p92, D3

This atmospheric cafe-restaurant in the crypt of one of London's most famous churches is breakfast and lunch only these days but offers excellent value and such tasty dishes as fish pie and Moroccan slow-roasted lamb in focaccia. There's always as many vegetarian choices as meat and fish ones. In summer there are tables outside on the shady courtyard. (www.cafebelow.co.uk; St Mary-le-Bow Church, Cheapside, EC2; mains £6.50-10; ⏰7.30am-2.30pm Mon-Fri; ✍; ⊖Mansion House)

White Swan Pub & Dining Room

GASTROPUB ££

15 ⊗ Map p92, A2

Though it may look like just another City pub from the street, the White Swan is anything but typical – it features a smart downstairs bar that serves excellent pub food under the watchful eyes of animal prints and trophies, and an upstairs dining room with a classic, meaty British menu (two-/three-course meal £27/31). (☏020-7242 9696; www.thewhiteswanlondon.com; 108 New Fetter Lane, EC4; mains £13-19.50; ⏰11am-11pm Mon, to midnight Tue-Thu, to 1am Fri; 🛜; ⊖Chancery Lane)

London Wall Bar & Kitchen

BRASSERIE ££

16 ⊗ Map p92, C2

Located right at the entrance of the Museum of London above London Wall, this brasserie makes inventive use of its meat supplies from nearby Smithfield Market, with everything from Spanish charcuterie to lamb kofta with apricots and harissa yoghurt on offer. (☏020-7600 7340; www.londonwallbarandkitchen.com; 150 London Wall, EC2; mains £9.50-15; ⏰11am-11pm Mon-Fri; ⊖Barbican, St Paul's)

Understand

The Great Fire of London

- -

With nearly all its buildings constructed from wood, London had for centuries been prone to conflagration, but it wasn't until 2 September 1666 that the mother of all blazes broke out, in a bakery in Pudding Lane in the City.

It didn't seem like much to begin with – the mayor himself dismissed it as being easily extinguished, before going back to bed – but the unusual September heat combined with rising winds sparked a tinderbox effect. The fire raged out of control for days, reducing some 80% of London to carbon. Only eight people died (officially at least), but most of London's medieval, Tudor and Jacobean architecture was destroyed. The fire was finally stopped (at Fetter Lane, on the very edge of London) by blowing up all the buildings in the inferno's path. It is hard to overstate the scale of the destruction – 89 churches and more than 13,000 houses were razed, leaving tens of thousands of people homeless. Many Londoners left for the countryside or sought their fortunes in the New World.

Wine Library

 MODERN EUROPEAN ££

17 Map p92, H4

This is a great place for a light but boozy lunch in the City. Buy a bottle of wine at retail price (no mark-up, £7.50 corkage fee) from the large selection on offer at the vaulted-cellar restaurant and then snack on a set plate of delicious pâtés, cheeses and salads. Reservations recommended for lunch. (☏020-7481 0415; www.winelibrary.co.uk; 43 Trinity Sq, EC3; set meal £17.50; ⊙11.30am-3pm Mon, to 8pm Tue-Fri; ⊖Tower Hill)

St John

BRITISH £££

18 Map p92, B1

This London classic is wonderfully simple – its light bar and cafe area give way to a surprisingly small dining room where 'nose to tail' eating is served up courtesy of celebrity chef Fergus Henderson. This was one of the places that launched Londoners on the quest to rediscover their culinary past. (☏020-7251 0848; www.stjohnrestaurant.com; 26 St John St, EC1; mains £17-23; ⊙noon-3pm & 6-11pm Mon-Sat, 1-3pm Sun; ⊖Farringdon)

Royal Exchange Grand Café & Bar

MODERN EUROPEAN ££

19 Map p92, E3

This lovely cafe-restaurant sits in the middle of the covered courtyard of the beautiful Royal Exchange building and is a good place to people-watch. The food runs the gamut from breakfast, salads and sandwiches to

Royal Exchange

oysters (from £11 a half-dozen) and rabbit cassoulet (£13.50). (☏020-7618 2480; www.royalexchange-grandcafe.co.uk; Royal Exchange, Bank, EC3; mains £13.50-22; ⊙8am-11pm Mon-Fri; ⊖Bank)

Drinking

Folly

BAR

20 Map p92, F4

Love, love, love this 'secret garden' bar-cum-cafe on two levels filled with greenery (both real and faux) and picnic-table seating. The aptly named Folly has a full menu on offer, with a strong emphasis on burgers and steaks, but we come for the excellent wine and Champagne selection. (www.

thefollybar.com; 41 Gracechurch St, EC3;
🕑7.30am-late Fri, from 10am Sat & Sun;
⊖Monument)

Vertigo 42   BAR

21 Map p92, F2

On the 42nd floor of a 183m-high
tower, this circular bar has expansive
views over the city that stretch for
miles on a clear day. The classic drinks
list is, as you might expect, pricier
than average – wine by the glass starts
at £9.50 and Champagne and cocktails from £14. Reservations essential;
minimum spend £10. (📞020-7877 7842;
www.vertigo42.co.uk; Tower 42, 25 Old Broad
St, EC2; 🕑noon-3.45pm Mon-Fri, 5-11pm Mon-
Sat; ⊖Liverpool St)

Fabric   CLUB

22 🚇 Map p92, B1

This most impressive of superclubs is
still the first stop on the London scene
for many international clubbers. The
crowd is hip and well dressed without
overkill, and the music – electro,
techno, house, drum and bass and
dubstep – is as superb as you'd expect
from London's top-rated club. (www.
fabriclondon.com; 77a Charterhouse St, EC1;
admission £8-18; 🕑10pm-6am Fri, 11pm-8am
Sat, 11pm-6am Sun; ⊖Farringdon)

Blackfriar   PUB

23 🚇 Map p92, B4

It may look like the corpulent friar
just stepped out of this 'olde pub' just
north of Blackfriars station, but the
interior is actually an Arts and Crafts

design makeover dating to 1905. It's
built on the site of a monastery of
Dominicans (who wore black), and
the theme is appealingly celebrated
throughout the pub. There's a good
selection of ales. (174 Queen Victoria St,
EC4; 🕑10am-11.30 Mon-Thu, to midnight Fri &
Sat, to 11pm Sun; ⊖Blackfriars)

Counting House   PUB

24 🚇 Map p92, F3

With its counters and basement
vaults, this award-winning pub
certainly looks and feels comfortable in the former headquarters of
NatWest Bank with its domed skylight
and beautifully appointed main bar.
This is a favourite of City boys and
girls – they come for the good range of
real ales and the speciality pies (from
£9.25). (50 Cornhill, EC3; 🕑11am-11pm Mon-
Fri; 📶; ⊖Bank, Monument)

Madison   COCKTAIL BAR

25 🚇 Map p92, D3

Perched atop One New Change with
a full-frontal view of St Paul's and
beyond, Madison offers one of the
largest public open-air roof terraces
you'll ever encounter. There's a full
restaurant on one side and a cocktail
bar with outdoor seating on the other;
we come for the latter and inventive
tapas (£4 to £14) such as popcorn
squid. (www.madisonlondon.net; Roof Terrace, One New Change, EC4; 🕑10am-midnight
Mon-Sat, to 8pm Sun; ⊖St Paul's)

Ye Olde Cheshire Cheese PUB

26 Map p92, A3

The entrance to this historic pub is via a narrow alley off Fleet St. Over its long history locals have included Dr Johnson, Thackeray and Dickens. Despite (or possibly because of) this, the Cheshire feels today like a bit of a museum. Nevertheless it's one of London's most famous pubs and it's well worth popping in for a pint. (Wine Office Court, 145 Fleet St, EC4; ⊙11am-11pm Mon-Fri, from noon Sat; ⊖Chancery Lane)

Entertainment

Barbican PERFORMING ARTS

27 ⭐ Map p92, D1

Home to the wonderful London Symphony Orchestra and its associate, the lesser-known BBC Symphony Orchestra, this arts centre hosts scores of other leading musicians each year as well, focusing in particular on jazz, folk, world and soul artists. Dance is another strong point. (☏0845 121 6823; www.barbican.org.uk; Silk St, EC2; ⊖Barbican)

Shopping

Spitalfields Market MARKET

28 Map p92, H1

One of London's best markets, with traders hawking their wares here since the early 17th century. The

covered market that you see today was built in the late 19th century, with the more modern development added in 2006. It is open six days a week, but Sundays are best and filled with fashion, jewellery, food and music stalls. (www.oldspitalfieldsmarket.com; Commercial St, btwn Brushfield & Lamb Sts, E1; ⊙10am-4pm Sun-Fri; ⊖Liverpool St)

London Silver Vaults SILVER

29 🔒 Map p92, A2

The 30 shops that work out of these incredibly secure subterranean vaults hold the largest collection of silver under one roof in the world. Everything from cutlery sets and picture frames to jewellery and tableware is on offer. (www.thesilvervaults.com; 53-63 Chancery Lane, WC2; ⊙9am-5.30pm Mon-Fri, to 1pm Sat; ⊖Chancery Lane)

Local Life
A Night out in Shoreditch

Getting There

🚃 Shoreditch High St and Hoxton are handy stops on the Overground.

🚇 Old St is a useful station, on the Northern Line (also by National Rail).

After a day's sightseeing, night owls can wing over to Shoreditch for a taste of its slick bars, cutting-edge clubs, funky restaurants and spot-on pubs catering to a local creative/media crowd fleeing high rents elsewhere. Once working class but now gentrified, the neighbourhood spills into hip Hoxton, where the night's partying continues.

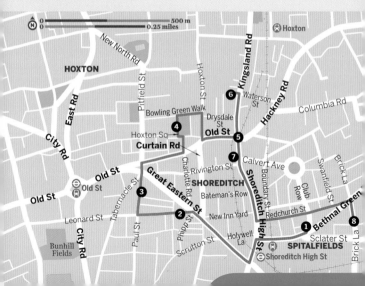

1 Dine at Les Trois Garçons

The name may prepare you for the French menu, but not the camp decor at this Victorian pub turned **restaurant** (☏020-7613 1924; www.lestroisgarcons. com; 1 Club Row, E1; mains £15-27; ⏱noon-2pm Thu & Fri, 6-9.30pm Mon-Thu, 6-10.30pm Fri & Sat; ⊖Shoreditch High St), complete with stuffed animals, chandeliers and suspended handbags.

2 Drink at Book Club

In a former warehouse, **Book Club** (☏020-7684 8618; www.wearetbc.com; 100 Leonard St; ⏱8am-midnight Mon-Wed, 8am-2am Thu & Fri, 10am-2am Sat & Sun; ☎; ⊖Old St) has offbeat events (spoken word, dance lessons, life drawing), as well as DJ nights (punk, ska and '60s pop to electro, house and disco). Food is available day and night.

3 Mingle with the Suits

Handsome and buzzing pub the **Princess of Shoreditch** (☏020-7729 9270; www.theprincessofshoreditch.com; 76 Paul St; pub mains £10-18.50; ⏱kitchen noon-3pm & 6.30-10pm Mon-Sat, noon-9pm Sun; ☎; ⊖Old St) is frequented by city suits and media types. Food is very well done, backed up by polite service, and a comprehensive wine and ale list.

4 Mix up a Cocktail

The menu at **Happiness Forgets** (☏020-7613 0325; www.happinessforgets. com; 8-9 Hoxton Sq, N1; ⏱5-11pm Mon-Sat; ☒Hoxton, ⊖Old St) promises mixed drinks and mischief at this basement bar with good-value cocktails.

5 Hit the Dance Floor

It doesn't look like much, but **Catch** (www.thecatchbar.com; 22 Kingsland Rd, E2; ⏱6pm-midnight Mon-Wed, to 2am Thu-Sat, 7pm-1am Sun; ⊖Old St, Shoreditch High St) is one of the best nights out in Shoreditch. Upstairs: '90s funk and hip-hop, or new and established bands. Downstairs: a big house-party vibe with DJs (free).

6 Get a Pick-Me-Up at Bridge

Late night caffeine? Upstairs at **Bridge** (15 Kingsland Rd, E2; ⏱noon-1am Sun-Thu, to 2am Fri & Sat; ☎; ⊖Old St, Hoxton) is a rococo salon-cum-boudoir that resembles something decorated by the bastard love child of Louis XIV and your eccentric auntie with all the cats. The downstairs bar retains an Italian theme with a fantastic old-fashioned till. It sells coffee and snacks.

7 Club It at Cargo

One of London's most eclectic clubs, **Cargo** (www.cargo-london.com; 83 Rivington St, EC2; admission free-£16; ⏱6pm-1am Mon-Thu, to 3am Fri & Sat, to midnight Sun; ⊖Old St) boasts a dance-floor room, bar and terrace. The music is innovative, with plenty of up-and-coming bands. Food is available throughout the day.

8 Grab a Late-Night Snack

Round off a full night with a bagel. You won't find fresher (or cheaper) bagels than at **Brick Lane Beigel Bake** (159 Brick Lane, E2; £1-4; ⏱24hr; ⊖Shoreditch High St, Liverpool St); just ask any taxi driver.

Explore

Tate Modern & South Bank

The South Bank has transformed into one of London's must-see neighbourhoods. A roll call of riverside sights lines the Thames, commencing with the London Eye, running past the cultural enclave of the Southbank Centre and on to the outstanding Tate Modern, Millennium Bridge, Shakespeare's Globe, waterside pubs, a cathedral and one of London's most-visited food markets.

The Sights in a Day

☀ Pre-booked ticket for the **London Eye** (p113) in hand, enjoy a leisurely revolution in the skies for astronomical city views (if the weather's clear). Hop on a bus to the **Imperial War Museum** (p112), where trench warfare, the Holocaust and London during the Blitz are brilliantly documented.

☀ Stop at the **Anchor & Hope** (p116) for lunch before making your way to the **Tate Modern** (p106). If you've a taste for modern art, the whole afternoon may vanish. Grab a photograph of St Paul's Cathedral on the far side of the elegant **Millennium Bridge** (p112) and consider a tour of the iconic **Shakespeare's Globe** (p112).

☾ Sink a drink in the historic **George Inn** (p118) on Borough High St or choose from the countless ales and ciders at **Rake** (p117) before devouring fresh fish at **Applebee's Fish Cafe** (p116). Theatre lovers will have tickets booked for the **National Theatre** (p119) or the **Old Vic** (p120).

 Top Sights

Tate Modern (p106)

💙 **Best of London**

Views

London Eye (p113)

Shard (p114)

Oxo Tower Restaurant & Brasserie (p117)

Skylon (p115)

Eating

Baltic (p115)

Skylon (p115)

Entertainment

Shakespeare's Globe (p119)

National Theatre (p119)

Southbank Centre (p120)

Getting There

⊖ **Tube** Waterloo, Southwark and London Bridge are on the Jubilee Line. London Bridge and Waterloo are also served by the Northern Line (and National Rail).

🚌 **Bus** The Riverside RV1 runs around the South Bank and Bankside, linking all the main sights.

Top Sights
Tate Modern

The public's love affair with this phenomenally successful modern-art gallery shows no sign of cooling more than a decade after it opened. In fact, so enraptured are art goers with the Tate Modern that more than 50 million visitors flocked to the former power station in its first 10 years. To accommodate this exceptional popularity, the Tate is expanding: the museum is creating new gallery space underground (in the former oil tanks) and above ground (with an 11-storey extension at the back). The grand opening is planned for 2016.

◉ Map p110, D2

www.tate.org.uk

Queen's Walk, SE1

admission free

⊙10am-6pm Sun-Thu, to 10pm Fri & Sat

⊖Southwark, St Paul's

Tate Modern, designed by Herzog & de Meuron

Don't Miss

Architecture

The 200m-long Tate Modern is an imposing sight. The conversion of the empty Bankside Power Station – all 4.2 million bricks of it – to an art gallery in 2000 was a design triumph. Leaving the building's single central 99m-high chimney, adding a two-storey glass box onto the roof and employing the cavernous Turbine Hall as a dramatic entrance space were three strokes of genius.

Turbine Hall

First to greet you as you pour down the ramp off Holland St (the main entrance) is the cavernous 3300-sq-metre Turbine Hall. It originally housed the power station's humungous turbines. Today the Turbine Hall is a commanding space that has housed some of the gallery's most famous temporary commissions such as Carsten Höller's funfair-like slides *Test Site* and Doris Salcedo's huge, enigmatic fissure *Shibboleth*.

Permanent Collection
LEVELS 2, 3 & 4

Tate Modern's permanent collection is arranged by theme and chronology. More than 60,000 works are on constant rotation, and the curators have at their disposal paintings by Georges Braque, Piet Mondrian, Andy Warhol, Mark Rothko and many more. This can be frustrating for those who are keen to see a particular work but means that every trip is unique.

HIGHLIGHTS

You've probably spotted all these masterpieces before in books and postcards, but seeing them for real is something else altogether. Look out for Matisse's signature collage *The Snail,* Picasso's

☑ Top Tips

▶ Free guided tours depart at 11am, noon, 2pm and 3pm daily.

▶ Audioguides (in five languages) are available for £4 – they contain explanations about 50 artworks across the galleries and offer suggested tours for adults or children.

▶ The Tate Modern is open late night Friday and Saturday (till 10pm).

▶ To go to the Tate Britain, hop on a boat.

▶ Connect to the gallery's free wi-fi and download their funky apps.

✕ Take a Break

The **Tate Modern Restaurant** (◷lunch Sun-Thu, lunch & dinner Fri & Sat) on level 6 is a good choice for a main meal, morning coffee or afternoon tea with panoramic vistas.

Or head to nearby Borough Market (p121) on Fridays and Saturdays for an alfresco lunch at one of the numerous food stalls.

distinctive *Weeping Woman,* Roy Lichtenstein's cartoon-like *Whaam!* or Salvador Dalí's surreal *Lobster Telephone.* Check with a member of staff whether a particular piece is on display.

Poetry & Dream
LEVEL 2

This collection submerges the viewer in the world of surrealism and the dreamlike mindscapes of Yves Tanguy, Max Ernst, Salvador Dalí, René Magritte and other artists. Search out *Sleeping Venus* by Paul Delvaux, a haunting, erotic work.

Tranformed Visions
LEVEL 3

After WWII, many artists channelled their emotions about war and violence in their works. One such manifestation was a new kind of expressive, contemplative abstraction, as exemplified by Mark Rothko's *The Seagram Murals.* The gallery also explores how human presence became a theme in the creative output of the post-war period and how depictions of it changed.

Understand
Tate of the Art

Swiss architects Herzog & de Meuron scooped the prestigious Pritzker Prize in 2001 for their transformation of the empty Bankside Power Station (built between 1947 and 1963 and shut by high oil prices in 1981). The conversion of the power station into a now-iconic art gallery displayed an inspired and visionary use of space and architecture.

The transformation continues with the construction of a daring 11-storey geometric extension at the back of the existing building. Also designed by Herzog & de Meuron, the extension will similarly be constructed of brick, but artistically devised as a lattice through which interior lights will be visible at night. Though not scheduled to open until 2016, the outline of the building will be distinguishable from 2014.

In July 2012, Tate Modern temporarily opened the two enormous, cavernous tanks that served as storage for the oil that fuelled the power station. The tanks will re-open permanently when the Tate's extension is completed; a pioneering art space (circular, raw, industrial) that will be dedicated to live art, performance and film installations.

The extension will give Tate Modern a chance to exhibit a lot more of its impressive collection. The gallery also wants to give pride of place to live art installations and large-scale pieces.

Tate Modern, designed by Herzog & de Meuron

The Evolution of Abstraction & Art
LEVEL 4

Focusing on the evolution of abstract art since the beginning of the 20th century, including cubism, geometric abstraction and minimalism, 'Structure & Clarity' includes work by early adopters such as Matisse and Picasso (*Seated Nude*). 'Energy & Process' highlights Arte Povera, a revolutionary Italian art movement from the 1960s, as its main focus.

Special Exhibitions
LEVELS 2 & 3

Special exhibitions (subject to admission charge, usually around £11) are one of the Tate Modern's drawcards and have included retrospectives on Edward Hopper, Frida Kahlo, Roy Lichtenstein, August Strindberg, Nazism and 'Degenerate' Art, and Joan Miró. Highlights for 2014 include blockbuster exhibitions on Matisse, JMW Turner and Piet Mondrian.

Views

The Tate Modern is in a prime location on the River Thames and sports divine views of St Paul's Cathedral on the north bank. This has become a signature London landscape so take time to take it all in from the balconies of the Espresso Bar (level 3) or with a cocktail in the panoramic level 6 bar.

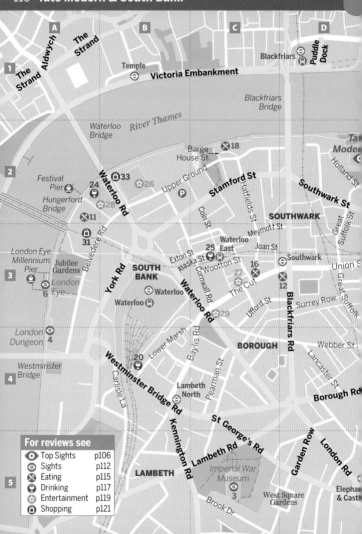

E — Queen Victoria St — Mansion House
Millennium Bridge
Shakespeare's Globe
1 — Bankside Pier
Bankside
Park St
Sumner St
Great Guildford St
Southwark Bridge Rd
pperfield St
thwark Bridge Rd — Lant St
Newington Causeway
Harper Rd
Trinity St
Falmouth Rd
Elephant & Castle

F — Cannon St
Cannon St
Queen St
Upper Thames St
Southwark Bridge
River Thames
Bankside
Clink St — Southwark
Montague Cl — Cathedral
Winchester Walk — 19 — 9
Stoney St — 30
15 — 5
Borough Market — London Bridge
21
Redcross Way
Borough — Borough High St
Newcomen St
Kipling St
Great Dover St
Law St
New Kent Rd

G — King William St — Gracechurch St
Monument
Old Billingsgate Market
London Bridge
Southwark Cathedral
Old Operating Theatre Museum & Herb Garret
London Bridge
8
Shard
St Thomas St
Weston St
Snowsfields
Leathermarket St — 22 — 17
32 — 23
BERMONDSEY — 13
Long La
Decima St
Rothsay St
Grange Rd
Pages Wlk

H — Fenchurch St
Byward St
Lower Thames St
Tower of London
HMS Belfast
7
London Bridge City Pier — The Queen's Walk
City Hall — 10
William Curtis Park
Tooley St
14
Crucifix La — Druid St
Tanner St
Bermondsey St
Tower Bridge Rd
Abbey St
Bermondsey Market

N — 0 — 500 m
0 — 0.25 miles

Sights

Shakespeare's Globe
HISTORIC BUILDING

1 Map p110, E2

Shakespeare's Globe consists of the authentically reconstructed outdoor Globe Theatre, the Sam Wanamaker winter (indoor!) playhouse and a fantastic exhibition hall. Tours of the playhouses fit around productions and are therefore not guaranteed. Check the schedule. (www.shakespearesglobe. com; 21 New Globe Walk, SE1; adult/child £13.50/8; ⏱9am-5.30pm; ⊖London Bridge)

Millennium Bridge
BRIDGE

2 Map p110, E1

The elegant Millennium Bridge staples the south bank of the Thames, in front of Tate Modern, with the north bank, at the steps of Peter's Hill below St Paul's Cathedral. The low-slung

Top Tip

London Eye Tickets

The London Eye draws 3.5 million visitors annually, and at peak times (July, August and school holidays) it can seem like every one of them is in the queue with you. Save money and shorten queues by buying tickets online, or cough up an extra £10 to showcase your fast-track swagger. Alternatively, visit before 11am or after 3pm to avoid peak density.

frame designed by Sir Norman Foster and Antony Caro looks spectacular, particularly lit up at night with fibre optics.

Imperial War Museum
MUSEUM

3 Map p110, C5

Fronted by a pair of intimidating 15in naval guns, this riveting museum is housed in what was once Bethlehem Royal Hospital, also known as Bedlam. Although the museum's focus is on military action involving British or Commonwealth troops during the 20th century, there are many references to war in the wider sense. (www. iwm.org.uk; Lambeth Rd, SE1; admission free; ⏱10am-6pm; ⊖Lambeth North)

London Dungeon
HISTORIC BUILDING

4 Map p110, A4

In a brand new home since March 2013, the Dungeon takes you on an entertaining whirlwind through London's most famous historical anecdotes – the gunpowder plot, the Great Plague, Jack the Ripper – narrated through a combination of rides, actors and special effects. There is great audience participation, but prepare to be scared and startled at every corner! (www.thedungeons.com/london; County Hall, Westminster Bridge Rd, SE1; adult/child £24.60/19.20; ⏱10am-5pm, extended hrs holidays; 🚻; ⊖Westminster, Waterloo)

CHRISTER FREDRIKSSON / GETTY IMAGES ©

Millennium Bridge to Tate Modern (p106)

Old Operating Theatre Museum & Herb Garret MUSEUM

5 Map p110, G2

This unique museum, 32 steps up the spiral stairway in the tower of St Thomas Church (1703), is the unlikely home of Britain's oldest operating theatre. Rediscovered in 1956, the garret was used by the apothecary of St Thomas Hospital to store medicinal herbs. The museum looks back at the horror of 19th-century medicine – all pre-ether, pre-chloroform and pre-antiseptic. (www.thegarret.org.uk; 9a St Thomas St, SE1; adult/child £6/3.50; 10.30am-5pm; London Bridge)

London Eye VIEWPOINT

6 Map p110, A3

The landmark 135m-tall London Eye fundamentally altered the South Bank skyline. A ride – or 'flight', as it is called here – in one of the wheel's 32 glass-enclosed eye pods, holding up to 28 people, takes a gracefully slow 30 minutes. Weather permitting, you can see 25 miles in every direction. (0871 781 3000; www.londoneye.com; adult/child £19.20/12.30; 10am-8pm; Waterloo)

HMS Belfast SHIP

7 Map p110, H2

Its white ensign flapping on the Thames breeze, HMS *Belfast* is a magnet for naval-gazing kids of all ages.

This large, light cruiser – launched in 1938 – served in WWII, helping to sink the German battleship *Scharnhorst,* shelling the Normandy coast on D Day and later participating in the Korean War. Its 6in guns could bombard a target 14 land miles distant. (hmsbelfast.iwm.org.uk; Queen's Walk, SE1; adult/child £14.50/free; ⏰10am-5pm; 🚻; ⬤London Bridge)

Shard

NOTABLE BUILDING

8 Map p110, G3

Puncturing the London skies, the dramatic splinter-like form of the Shard has rapidly become an icon of the town. The viewing platforms on floors 68, 69 and 72 are open to the public and the views are, as you'd expect from a 244m vantage point, sweeping, but they come at a hefty price – book online to save £5. (www.the-shard.com; 32 London Bridge St, SE1; adult/child £29.95/23.95; ⏰9am-10pm; ⬤London Bridge)

 Top Tip

Walking the South Bank

The drawcard sights stretch west–east in a manageable riverside melange, so doing it on foot is the best way. To collect the main sights along the South Bank, trace the Silver Jubilee Walk and the South Bank section of the Thames Path along the riverbank, with occasional inroads inland for shopping, dining and drinking.

Understand

Bridge Troubles

The Millennium Bridge got off on the wrong footing when it was closed just three days after opening in June 2000 due to an alarming swing. A costly 18-month refit put things right.

Southwark Cathedral

CHURCH

9 Map p110, F2

Although the central tower dates from 1520 and the choir from the 13th century, Southwark Cathedral is largely Victorian. Inside are monuments galore, including a Shakespeare Memorial. Catch evensong at 5.30pm on Tuesdays, Thursdays and Fridays, 4pm on Saturdays and 3pm on Sundays. (☎020-7367 6700; cathedral.southwark.anglican.org; Montague Close, SE1; donations welcome; ⏰8am-6pm Mon-Fri, from 9am Sat & Sun; ⬤London Bridge)

City Hall

NOTABLE BUILDING

10 Map p110, H2

Office of the Mayor of London, bulbous City Hall was designed by Foster and Partners and opened in 2002. The 45m, glass-clad building has been compared to a host of objects – from an onion, to Darth Vader's helmet, a woodlouse and a 'glass gonad'. (www.london.gov.uk; Queen's Walk, SE1; ⬤London Bridge)

Eating

Skylon
MODERN EUROPEAN ££

11 Map p110, A2

Named after the defunct 1950s tower, this excellent restaurant on top of the refurbished Royal Festival Hall is divided into grill and fine-dining sections by a large bar (p117) (open until 1am). The decor is cutting-edge 1950s: muted colours and period chairs (trendy then, trendier now) while floor-to-ceiling windows bathe you in magnificent views of the Thames and the City. (☑020-7654 7800; www.skylonrestaurant.co.uk; 3rd fl, Royal Festival Hall, Southbank Centre, Belvedere Rd, SE1; grill mains £13-25, restaurant 2-/3-course menu £42/47.50; ☺grill noon-11pm; restaurant noon-2.30pm & 5.30-10.30pm Mon-Sat, noon-4pm Sun; ☻Waterloo)

Baltic
EASTERN EUROPEAN ££

12 Map p110, D3

In a bright and airy, high-ceilinged dining room with glass roof and wooden beams, Baltic is travel on a plate: dill and beetroot, dumplings and blini, pickle and smoke, rich stews and braised meat. From Poland to Georgia, the flavours are authentic and the dishes beautifully presented. The wine and vodka lists are equally diverse. (www.balticrestaurant.co.uk; 74 Blackfriars Rd; mains £9.50-18.50; ☺noon-3pm & 5.30-11.15pm Mon-Sat, to 10.30pm Sun; ☻Southwark)

Local Life
Maltby Street Market
This rollicking little **market** (www.maltby.st; Maltby St, SE1; ☺10am-4pm Sat; ☻London Bridge), nicknamed the Ropewalk, is a true gem. Started as an alternative to the juggernaut that is Borough Market, it is a small, rough-on-the-edges, bunting-lined gathering of small producers and boutique food stalls. Londoners love coming here to while away their Saturday afternoon.

Zucca
ITALIAN ££

13 Map p110, H4

In a crisp, minimalist dining room with wrap-around bay windows and an open kitchen, an (almost) all-Italian staff serves contemporary Italian fare. The pasta is made daily on the premises and the menu is kept deliberately short to promote freshness. (☑020-7873 6809; www.zuccalondon.com; 184 Bermondsey St; mains £15-18; ☺noon-3pm Tue-Sun, 6-10pm Tue-Sat; ☻London Bridge)

Magdalen
MODERN BRITISH ££

14 Map p110, H3

You can't go wrong with this formal dining room. The Modern British fare adds its own appetising spin to familiar dishes (grilled calves' kidneys, creamed onion and sage, smoked haddock *choucroute*); the desserts and English cheese selection are another delight. The welcome is warm and the service excellent. (📞020-7403 1342; www.magdalenrestaurant.co.uk; 152 Tooley St, SE1; mains £17-18, lunch 2-/3-course £15.50/18.50; ⏱noon-2.30pm Mon-Fri, 6.30-10pm Mon-Sat; 🚇London Bridge)

Applebee's Fish Cafe SEAFOOD ££

15 🍴 Map p110, F2

This excellent fishmonger with a cafe-restaurant attached serves all manner of fresher-than-fresh fish and shellfish dishes. And if nothing takes your fancy on the menu, the chef will happily cook the fish of your choice from the counter. (📞020-7407 5777; www.applebeesfish.com; 5 Stoney St, SE1; mains £15.50-25.50; ⏱noon-3.30pm & 6-11pm Tue-Sat; 🚇London Bridge)

Local Life
Pie & Mash

Those curious to find out how Londoners once ate before everything went chic and ethnic should visit a traditional pie 'n' mash shop. **M Manze** (Map p110, H5; www.manze.co.uk; 87 Tower Bridge Rd, SE1; ⏱11am-2pm Mon-Thu, 10am-2.30pm Fri & Sat; 🚇Borough) dates to 1902 and is a classic operation, from the lovely tile work to the traditional worker's menu: pie and mash (£3.40) or pie and liquor (£2.40), and you can take your eels jellied or stewed (£3.50).

Anchor & Hope PUB ££

16 🍴 Map p110, C3

The hope is that you'll get a table without waiting hours because you can't book at this quintessential gastropub. The anchor is gutsy, British food. Critics love this place inside out and despite the menu's heavy hitters (pork shoulder, salt marsh lamb shoulder cooked for seven hours, soy-braised shin of beef), vegetarians aren't completely stranded. (36 The Cut, SE1; mains £12-20; ⏱noon-2.30pm Tue-Sat, 6-10.30pm Mon-Sat, from 2pm Sun; 🚇Southwark)

Garrison Public House GASTROPUB ££

17 🍴 Map p110, H4

The Garrison's traditional green-tiled exterior and rather distressed, beach-shack interior are both appealing. It boasts an actual cinema (free films every Sunday at 7pm, intermission for drinks provided) in its basement, but it's the food (razor clams, black-face lamb gigot with roast squash, and pumpkin, chickpea and courgette cake) that lures punters to this ever-green Bermondsey gastropub. (www.thegarrison.co.uk; 99-101 Bermondsey St, SE1; mains £8.50-17; ⏱8-11am, 12.30-3pm & 6-10pm; 🚇London Bridge)

The Cut BRITISH £

This all-day brasserie at the front of the Young Vic theatre (see 27 ✪ Map p110) has put sustainability at the heart of its menu: organic beef burgers, free-range chicken breast in spices and lime, sustainably sourced pan-fried sea bass – and freshly made salads and cakes. The Triple Cut lunch deal (Monday to Thursday) with burger and drink for £8.95 is a snip. (www.thecutbar.com; Young Vic, The Cut, SE1; mains £7-12; ⏱9am-11pm Mon-Fri, 10am-11pm Sat; 🛜✏️; ⊖Waterloo)

Oxo Tower Restaurant & Brasserie

FUSION £££

18 🍴 Map p110, C2

Oxo Tower Restaurant & Brasserie

The iconic Oxo Tower's conversion, with this restaurant on the 8th floor, helped spur much of the local dining renaissance. In the stunning glassed-in terrace you have a front-row seat for the best view in London, and you pay for this handsomely in the brasserie and stratospherically in the restaurant. (📞020-7803 3888; www.harveynichols.com/restaurants/oxo-tower-london; Barge House St, SE1; mains £21.50-35; ⏱restaurant noon-2.30pm & 6-11pm, brasserie noon-11pm; ✏️; ⊖Waterloo)

Drinking

Skylon

BAR

With its 1950s decor and show-stopping views, Skylon (see **11** 🗺 Map p110, A2) is a memorable place for a drink. You'll have to come early to bag the tables at the front with plunging views of the river. Drinks-wise, just ask: from seasonal cocktails to a staggering choice of whiskys (and whiskeys!), you'll finish the night in high spirits. (www.skylon-restaurant.co.uk; Royal Festival Hall, Southbank Centre, Belvedere Rd, SE1; ⏱noon-1am Mon-Sat, to 10.30pm Sun; ⊖Waterloo)

Rake

PUB

19 🍺 Map p110, F2

The Rake offers more than 100 beers at any one time. The selection of bitters, real ales, lagers and ciders (with one-third pint measures) changes constantly. It's a tiny place yet always busy; the bamboo-decorated decking outside is especially popular. (www.uttobeer.co.uk; 14 Winchester Walk, SE1; ⏱noon-11pm Mon-Sat, to 8pm Sun; ⊖London Bridge)

Top Tip

Beg, Steal or Borough

Freeloaders, gastronomic bargain-hunters and the irrepressibly peckish need to make a pilgrimage to Borough Market (p121) when the munchies strike: loads of free samples can be had from the stalls – from tasty titbits to exotic fare.

Scootercaffe

CAFE, BAR

20 Map p110, B4

A real find in the elephants' graveyard we like to call Waterloo, this funky cafe-bar and former scooter repair shop with a Piatti scooter in the window serves killer hot chocolate, coffee and decadent cocktails. Unusually, you're allowed to bring take-away food. The tiny patio at the back is perfect for soaking up the sun. (132 Lower Marsh, SE1; ⏰8am-11pm Mon-Thu, to midnight Fri & Sat; 🛜; ⊖Waterloo)

George Inn

PUB

21 Map p110, F3

This magnificent old boozer is London's last surviving galleried coaching inn, dating from 1676 and mentioned in Dickens' *Little Dorrit*. It is on the site of the Tabard Inn, where the pilgrims in Chaucer's *Canterbury Tales* gathered before setting out (well lubricated, we suspect) on the road to Canterbury, Kent. (www.nationaltrust.org.uk/george-inn; 77 Borough High St, SE1; ⏰11am-11pm; ⊖London Bridge)

Woolpack

PUB

22 Map p110, H4

This free house (a pub that doesn't belong to a brewery) is a crowd pleaser: the British food is good, the decor lovely – dark-wood panels downstairs, Victorian wallpaper upstairs – the garden spacious, and it shows football and rugby games. (www.woolpackbar.com; 98 Bermondsey St; ⏰11am-11pm Mon-Sat, to 10.30pm Sun; ⊖London Bridge)

Street Coffee

CAFE

23 Map p110, H4

With its distressed sofas, house music and punk-meets-vintage-chic decor, Street Coffee is no ordinary cafe. The crowd is young, equipped with smartphones or laptops, and keen to be seen enjoying the lattes, smoothies, soups and sandwiches. (www.streetcoffee.co.uk; 163-167 Bermondsey St; ⏰7am-7pm Mon-Fri, 8am-8pm Sat & Sun; 🛜; ⊖London Bridge)

Queen Elizabeth Roof Garden

CAFE, BAR

24 Map p110, A2

Amidst the concrete jungle of the Queen Elizabeth Hall and the Hayward Gallery is this unexpected rooftop garden cafe-bar. The AstroTurf, colourful metal chairs, potted trees and planted 'wild meadows' make a disarming contrast with the surroundings, and the river views add to the sense of wonder. It's just a shame the drinks are so expensive... (Queen Elizabeth Hall, Southbank Centre, Belvedere Rd; ⏰10am-10pm Apr-Sep; ⊖Waterloo)

Swan at the Globe   BAR

At Shakespeare's Globe (see 1 ⭐ Map p110, E2) this fine pub-bar at the piazza level, with brasserie, is open for lunch and dinner (lunch only on Sunday). It has simply glorious views of the Thames and St Paul's from the 1st floor. (www.swanattheglobe.co.uk; 21 New Globe Walk, SE1; ⏱7.30am-11.30pm Mon-Thu, to 12.30am Fri & Sat, to 10.30pm Sun; ⊖London Bridge)

King's Arms   PUB

25 ⭕ Map p110, C3

Relaxed and charming when not crowded, this award-winning neighbourhood boozer at the corner of a terraced Waterloo backstreet was a funeral parlour in a previous life. The large traditional bar area, serving a good selection of ales and bitters, gives way to a fantastically odd conservatory bedecked with junk-store eclectica of local interest. It serves decent Thai food. (www.windmilltaverns.com; 25 Roupell St, SE1; ⏱11am-11pm Mon-Fri, noon-midnight Sat, noon-10.30pm Sun; ⊖Waterloo, Southwark)

Entertainment

National Theatre   THEATRE

26 ⭐ Map p110, B2

England's flagship theatre showcases a mix of classic and contemporary plays performed by excellent casts in three theatres (Olivier, Lyttelton and Cottesloe). Outstanding artistic director Nicholas Hytner (who will step down in March 2015) has overseen a golden decade at the theatre, with landmark productions such as *War Horse*, and there are constant surprises in the program. (☑020-7452 3000; www.nationaltheatre.org.uk; South Bank, SE1; ⊖Waterloo)

Shakespeare's Globe   THEATRE

This authentic Shakespearean theatre (see 1 ⭐ Map p110, E2) is a wooden O without a roof over the central stage area, and although there are covered wooden bench seats in tiers around the stage, many people (there's room for 700) do as 17th-century 'groundlings' did, and stand in front of the stage. (☑020-7401 9919; www.shakespearesglobe.com; 21 New Globe Walk, SE1; seats £15-42, standing £5; ⊖St Paul's, London Bridge)

○ Local Life
Festivals on the Thames

Numerous festivals take place in and around the Southbank Centre (p120). Our favourites include **Wonderground** (dedicated to circus and cabaret), **Udderbelly** (a comedy festival in all its guises – stand up, music, mime etc) and **Meltdown** (a music event curated by the best and most eclectic names in music – Yoko Ono in 2013, Massive Attack in 2008). Tickets are always available last minute.

Young Vic
THEATRE

27 ⭐ Map p110

This ground-breaking theatre is as much about discovering new talent as it is about discovering theatre. The Young Vic showcases actors, directors and plays from across the world, many of which tackle contemporary political or cultural issues such as the death penalty, racism or corruption, often blending dance and music with acting. (☏020-7922 2922; www.youngvic.org; 66 The Cut, SE1; ⊖Waterloo)

Southbank Centre
CONCERT HALL

28 ⭐ Map p110, B2

The overhauled Royal Festival Hall is one of London's premier concert venues and seats 3000. It's one of the best places for catching world and classical music artists. The sound is fantastic, the programming impeccable and there are frequent free gigs in the wonderfully expansive foyer. (☏020-7960 4200; www.southbankcentre.co.uk; Belvedere Rd, SE1; ⊖Waterloo)

Old Vic
THEATRE

29 ⭐ Map p110, C3

Never has there been a London theatre with a more famous artistic director. American actor Kevin Spacey took the theatrical helm in 2003, looking after this glorious theatre's program. The theatre does both new and classic plays, and its cast and directors are consistently high profile. (☏0844 871 7628; www.oldvictheatre.com; The Cut, SE1; ⊖Waterloo)

Understand

A Bard's Eye View of Shakespearian Theatre

The original Globe – known as the 'Wooden O' after its circular shape and roofless centre – was erected in 1599. The theatre burned to the ground in under two hours during a performance of a play about Henry VIII in 1613 (a stage cannon ignited the thatched roof). A tiled replacement was speedily rebuilt only to be closed in 1642 by Puritans, who saw the theatre as the devil's workshop. It was dismantled two years later.

The new Globe was the brainchild of American film director and actor Sam Wanamaker and was designed to resemble the original as closely as possible, painstakingly constructed with 600 oak pegs (nary a nail or a screw in the house), specially fired Tudor bricks and thatching reeds from Norfolk. Even the plaster contains goat hair, lime and sand as it did in Shakespeare's time. It does mean exposing the arena to the fickle London skies and roar of passing aircraft, leaving the 700 'groundlings' to stand in the open, even in London's notorious downpours.

Shopping

Borough Market

MARKET

30 Map p110, F2

'London's Larder' has occupied this spot in some form or another since the 13th century. The market has enjoyed an enormous renaissance in recent years, overflowing with food-lovers, both experienced and wannabe, and has become quite a tourist destination. (www.boroughmarket.org.uk; cnr Southwark & Stoney Sts, SE1; ⊘11am-5pm Thu, noon-6pm Fri, 8am-5pm Sat; ⊖London Bridge)

Southbank Centre Shop

DESIGN

31 Map p110, A3

This is the place to come for quirky London books, '50s-inspired home-wares, original prints and creative gifts for children. The shop is rather eclectic but you're sure to find unique gifts or souvenirs to take home. (www.southbankcentre.co.uk; Festival Tce; ⊘10am-9pm Mon-Fri, to 8pm Sat, noon-8pm Sun; ⊖Waterloo)

Lovely & British

DESIGN

32 Map p110, H4

This boutique prides itself on stocking work from British designers, including prints, jewellery and home furnishings. It's a mix of vintage and new, with reasonable prices. (132a Bermondsey St; ⊘11.30am-6pm Mon-Fri, 10am-5.30pm Sat, noon-4pm Sun; ⊖London Bridge)

ROB MACDOUGALL/GETTY IMAGES ©

Royal Festival Hall, Southbank Centre

Southbank Book Market

MARKET

33 Map p110, B2

Prints and secondhand books for sale daily under the arches of Waterloo Bridge. (Riverside Walk, SE1; ⊘11am-7pm, shorter hrs in winter; ⊖Waterloo)

Top Sights
Hampton Court Palace

Getting There

🚆 Regular services from Waterloo to Hampton Court, via Wimbledon station.

⛴ Westminster Passenger Services Association (www.wpsa.co.uk) runs boats from Westminster Pier.

London's most spectacular Tudor palace, 16th-century Hampton Court Palace is steeped in history, from the grand living quarters of Henry VIII to the spectacular gardens, complete with a 300-year-old maze. One of the best days out London has to offer, the palace is mandatory for anyone with an interest in British history, Tudor architecture or gorgeous landscaped gardens. Set aside plenty of time to do it justice (if you arrive by boat from central London, half the day will have vanished already).

Hampton Court Palace

Don't Miss

Clock Court
Passing through the magnificent main gate (Trophy Gate) you arrive first in the Base Court and then the Clock Court, named after the 16th-century astronomical clock that still shows the sun revolving round the earth. The second court is your starting point; from here you can follow any or all of the six sets of rooms in the complex.

Henry VIII's State Apartments
The stairs inside Anne Boleyn's Gateway lead up to Henry VIII's State Apartments, including the Great Hall, the largest single room in the palace, decorated with tapestries and what is considered the country's finest hammer-beam roof. The Horn Room, hung with impressive antlers, leads to the Great Watching Chamber where guards control-led access to the king.

Chapel Royal
Further along the corridor is the beautiful Chapel Royal, built in just nine months and still a place of worship after 450 years. The blue-and-gold vaulted ceiling was originally intended for Christ Church, Oxford, but was installed here instead. The 18th-century reredos was carved by Grinling Gibbons.

Royal Pew & Henry VIII's Crown
Henry VIII's dazzling gemstone-encrusted crown has been recreated – the original was melted down by Oliver Cromwell – and sits in the Royal Pew (open 10am to 4pm Monday to Saturday and 12.30pm to 1.30pm Sunday), which overlooks the beautiful Chapel Royal.

---

www.hrp.org.uk/
HamptonCourtPalace

adult/child
£17.60/8.80

⊙10am-6pm Apr-Oct,
10am-4.30pm Nov-Mar

⬙Hampton Court Pal-ace, ⬙Hampton Court

☑ Top Tips

▶ Glide (or slide) around the palace's glittering ice rink from late November to mid-January.

▶ Tag along with a cos-tumed guide on fun and informative tours.

✗ Take a Break

The palace's gorgeous gardens are an excellent place for picnicking.

The **Tiltyard Café** (Hampton Court Palace; ⊙10am-4.30pm Nov–late Mar, 10am-6pm late Mar–Oct) has a decent menu and lovely views over the garden.

Tudor Kitchens

The delightful Tudor kitchens, again accessible from Anne Boleyn's Gateway, once rustled up meals for a royal household of some 600 people. The kitchens have been fitted out as they might have appeared in Tudor days. Don't miss the Great Wine Cellar, which handled the 300 barrels each of ale and wine consumed here annually in the mid-16th century.

King's Apartments

West of the colonnade in the Clock Court is the entrance to the Wolsey Rooms and the Young Henry VIII exhibition. East of the colonnade in the Clock Court are stairs to the King's Apartments, a tour of which takes you up the grand King's Staircase, painted by Antonio Verrio. Highlights are the King's Great Bedchamber and the King's Closet (where His Majesty's toilet has a velvet seat).

Queen's Apartments

William's wife, Mary II, had her own Queen's Apartments, accessible up the Queen's Staircase, decorated by William Kent. When Mary died in 1694, work on the rooms was incomplete; they were finished during the reign of George II. Compared with the King's Apartments, those for the queen seem austere. At the time of writing, the apartments were being prepared for a new exhibition on the royal bedchamber.

Georgian Rooms

Also worth seeing are the Georgian Rooms used by George II and Queen Caroline on the last royal visit to the palace in 1737. Do not miss the fabulous Tudor Wolsey Closet with its early 16th-century ceiling and painted panels, commissioned by Henry VIII.

Cartoon Gallery

This is where the real Raphael Cartoons (now in the Victoria & Albert Museum) used to hang; the ones you see today in the Cartoon Gallery are late-17th-century copies.

Mantegna's Triumph of Caesar

Andrea Mantegna's nine huge and vivid Renaissance paintings depict a triumphant Julius Caesar arriving in Ancient Rome. The paintings are on display from 10.30am to 12.30pm and 1.30pm to 4pm.

Garden

Beyond the palace are the stunning gardens. Look out for the Real Tennis Court, dating from the 1620s. In the restored 24-hectare Riverside Gardens, you'll find the Great Vine, planted in 1768 and still producing just under 320kg of grapes per year.

Maze

No-one should leave Hampton Court without losing themselves in the 800m-long maze, made of hornbeam and yew, and planted in 1690. The maze is included in the palace entry fee; those not visiting the palace can enter the maze for £4.40 (£2.75/13.20 for children/families).

Understand

History of Hampton Court

Palace Origins

Like so many royal residences, Hampton Court Palace was not built for the monarchy at all. In 1515 Cardinal Thomas Wolsey, Lord Chancellor of England, built himself a palace in keeping with his sense of self-importance. Unfortunately, even Wolsey couldn't persuade the pope to grant Henry VIII a divorce from Catherine of Aragon, and relations between king and chancellor soured. With that in mind, you only need to glance at the palace to see why Wolsey felt obliged to present it to Henry, a monarch not too fond of anyone trying to outdo him. The hapless Wolsey was charged with high treason but died in 1530, before he could come to trial.

As soon as he had his royal hands upon the palace, Henry set to work expanding it, adding the Great Hall, the exquisite Chapel Royal and the sprawling kitchens. By 1540 it had become one of the grandest and most sophisticated palaces in Europe, but Henry only spent an average of three weeks a year here. In later years James I kept things ticking over at Hampton Court while Charles I put in a new tennis court and did some serious art collecting, before finding himself a prisoner in the palace during the Civil War. After the war, puritanical Oliver Cromwell warmed to his own regal proclivities, spending weekends in the comfort of the former Queen's bedroom at the palace and flogging Charles I's art collection. In the late 17th century, William and Mary employed Sir Christopher Wren for extensions: the result is a beautiful blend of Tudor and 'restrained baroque' architecture.

Haunted Hampton

With a history as old and as eventful as Hampton Court Palace, a paranormal dimension is surely par for the course. Arrested for adultery and detained in the palace in 1542, Henry's fifth wife, Catherine Howard, was dragged screaming down a gallery at the palace by her guards after an escape bid. Her ghost is said to do a repeat performance to this day in the Haunted Gallery (she must be a tireless ghost as she also haunts the Tower of London). Not to be outshone, the ghostly Grey Lady (supposedly former Tudor servant Dame Sybil Penn) has scared the bejesus out of mere mortals in the Clock Court and the State Apartments.

Explore

Kensington Museums

With its triumvirate of top museums, Kensington is compulsory sightseeing land. Shoppers will adore the King's Rd, mixing with the well-heeled up to Knightsbridge and Harrods via Sloane St, but also earmark a sight-packed day that includes a visit to Hyde Park and conjoined Kensington Gardens. Dining is an experience in itself, with astonishing choice, whether you're grazing or feasting.

The Sights in a Day

☀ Make a start with the bountiful **Victoria & Albert Museum** (p128), bearing in mind you could easily spend the entire day in this one museum alone. If you have children, start instead with the **Natural History** (p132) or **Science Museum** (p140), both enthralling for young ones. For lunch, dine at **Refreshment Rooms** at the V&A.

☀ Burn off your lunch by exploring central London's glorious green expanses: **Hyde Park** (p140) and **Kensington Gardens** (p140) will delight adults and children with their galleries, play areas and Kensington Palace. If you fancy a spot of shopping, you're in the right place: walk the length and breadth of **Old Brompton Rd**, with a compulsory stop at **Harrods** (p147).

☽ Dinner at **Launceston Place** (p143) or **Zuma** (p144) is highly recommended, but aim for sunset with a cocktail at **Galvin at Windows** (p145) or rub shoulders with local drinkers at the **Drayton Arms** (p145). Tickets for a performance at the **Royal Albert Hall** (p146) or the **Royal Court Theatre** (p146) will conclude a sightseeing-packed day with a much needed seat and great entertainment.

For a local's day in Kensington, see p136.

◉ Top Sights

Victoria & Albert Museum (p128)

Natural History Museum (p132)

◐ Local Life

Shopping in Chelsea & Knightsbridge (p136)

♥ Best of London

Eating

Launceston Place (p143)

Dinner by Heston Blumenthal (p143)

Shops

Harrods (p147)

Harvey Nichols (p137)

John Sandoe Books (p137)

For Kids

Science Museum (p140)

Natural History Museum (p132)

Getting There

◉ **Tube** Hyde Park Corner, Knightsbridge and South Kensington (Piccadilly Line) and South Kensington, Sloane Sq and High St Kensington (Circle & District Lines).

🚌 **Bus** Handy routes include 74, 52 and 360.

Top Sights
Victoria & Albert Museum

Specialising in decorative art and design, the museum universally known as the V&A hosts some 4.5 million objects reaching back as far as 3000 years, from Britain and around the globe. This unparalleled collection is displayed in a setting as inspiring as the sheer diversity and (often exquisite) rarity of its exhibits.

V&A

Map p138, D4

www.vam.ac.uk

Cromwell Rd, SW7

admission free

10am-5.45pm Sat-Thu, to 10pm Fri

South Kensington

Sculptures in the British Galleries, Victoria & Albert Museum

Don't Miss

Islamic Middle East Gallery
ROOM 42, LEVEL 1

This gallery holds more than 400 objects from the Islamic Middle East, including ceramics, textiles, carpets, glass and woodwork from the 8th-century caliphate up to the years before WWI.

Ardabil Carpet
ROOM 42, LEVEL 1

The highlight of the Islamic Middle East Gallery is the gorgeous Ardabil Carpet, the world's oldest dated carpet (and one of the largest). It was completed in 1540, one of a pair commissioned by Shah Tahmasp, then ruler of Iran. The carpet is most astonishing for the artistry of the detailing and the breathtaking subtlety of its design.

China Collection & the Japan Gallery
ROOMS 44, 45 & 47E, LEVEL 1

The TT Tsui China collection (rooms 44 and 47e) displays lovely pieces, including an art deco woman's jacket (1925–35) and exquisite Tang dynasty Sancai porcelain. Within the subdued lighting of the Japan Gallery (room 45) stands a fearsome suit of armour in the Domaru style.

Tipu's Tiger
ROOM 41, LEVEL 1

This disquieting 18th-century wood-and-metal mechanical automaton portrays a European being savaged by a tiger. When a handle is turned, an organ hidden within the feline mimics the cries of the dying man, whose arm also rises.

Cast Courts
ROOM 46A, LEVEL 1

One of the museum's highlights is the Cast Courts, containing staggering plaster casts collected in

☑ Top Tips

▶ For fewer crowds and more space, visit late on Friday evenings.

▶ Free introductory guided tours leave the main reception area at 10.30am, 12.30pm, 1.30pm and 3.30pm.

▶ The V&A's temporary exhibitions are compelling and fun (admission fees apply).

▶ The museum hosts great talks, workshops and events and has one of the best museum shops around.

▶ For fresh air, the landscaped John Madejski Garden is a lovely shaded inner courtyard.

✖ Take a Break

Make for the **V&A Café** (V&A; ⏱10am-5.15pm Sat-Thu, to 9.30pm Fri) in the magnificent Refreshment Rooms (Morris, Gamble and Poynter Rooms), dating from the 1860s.

In the summer, the **Garden Café** in the John Madejski Garden is open for drinks and snacks.

the Victorian era, such as Michelangelo's *David*, acquired in 1858.

Photographs Gallery
ROOM 100, LEVEL 3

The V&A was the first museum in the world to collect photographs as art. It is therefore not surprising that its photography collection is one of the best anywhere, with more than 500,000 images collected since 1856.

Raphael Cartoons
48A, LEVEL 1

The highly celebrated Raphael cartoons, which were moved here from Hampton Court Palace in 1865, are designs for tapestries created for the Sistine Chapel.

Fashion Galleries
ROOM 40, LEVEL 1

Beautifully refurbished in 2011, this is among the most popular exhibits, with displays of European fashion, fabrics and accessories from 1750 to the present day. Highlights include 18th-century gowns, Vivienne Westwood pieces, and designs from contemporary catwalks.

Henry VIII's Writing Box
ROOM 58E, LEVEL 2

The British Galleries, featuring every aspect of British design from 1500 to 1900, are divided between levels 2 (1500–1760) and 4 (1760–1900). One highlight is a relic from Henry VIII's reign – an exquisitely ornate walnut and oak 16th-century writing box. The original decorative motifs are superb, including Henry's coat of arms, flanked by Venus (holding Cupid) and Mars.

Great Bed of Ware
ROOM 57, LEVEL 2

There's also the so-called Great Bed of Ware from the late 16th century, big enough to sleep five! With an astounding width of 326cm, the bed even finds mention in William Shakespeare's *Twelfth Night*.

Hereford Screen
LEVEL 3

Designed by Sir George Gilbert Scott, this mighty choir screen is a labour of love, originally fashioned for Hereford Cathedral. It's an almighty conception of wood, iron, copper, brass and hardstone, and few parts of the museum could support its terrific mass.

Jewellery Gallery
ROOMS 91–93, LEVEL 3

The Jewellery Gallery in Materials and Techniques is outstanding, including pieces of exquisite intricacy from early Egyptian, Greek and Roman jewellery to dazzling tiaras and contemporary designs. The upper level – accessed via a glass and perspex spiral staircase – glitters with jewel-encrusted swords, watches and gold boxes.

20th Century Gallery
ROOMS 74–76, LEVEL 3

The 20th Century Gallery embraces design classics from a Le Corbusier chaise longue to a Sony Walkman, Katherine Hamnett T-shirts and a Nike 'Air Max' shoe from 1992.

Understand

Intriguing History

The V&A opened in 1852 on the back of the runaway success of the Great Exhibition of 1851 and Prince Albert's enthusiasm for the arts. Its aims were to make art available to all, and to effect 'improvement of public taste in design'. It began with objects first collected by the Government School of Design in the 1830s and '40s, and £5000 worth of purchases thanks to profits from the Great Exhibition.

Architectural Pains

The Museum of Manufactures, as it was then known, moved its eclectic mix of designs and innovations to South Kensington in 1857, to a collection of semi-permanent buildings. An expansion brought more ad hoc structures, and in 1890 the museum's board launched a competition to design the museum's new facade on Cromwell Rd and bring harmony to its architectural hotchpotch. Young architect Aston Webb (who went on to build the facade of Buckingham Palace) won and Queen Victoria laid the foundation stone in May 1899. The occasion marked a name change: it was now called the Victoria & Albert Museum.

Thwarting the Suffragettes

In 1913, suffragettes threatened to vandalise the museum's priceless treasures. Rather than banning women, the V&A decided instead to drop admission fees to increase the number of visitors, which would provide added security for the collection. It also introduced temporary measures demanding that umbrellas and sticks be left at the entrance (and ladies' muffs 'discreetly' checked at the door).

V&A in the Wars

The V&A remained open during both world wars. When WWI broke out, several of French sculptor Auguste Rodin's works were on loan at the V&A, and the hostilities prevented their return to France. Rodin was so moved by the solidarity of English and French troops that he donated the pieces to the museum. During WWII, the museum was hit repeatedly by German bombs (a commemorative inscription remains on Cromwell Rd). Much of the collection had been evacuated (or bricked in, as with Raphael's cartoons) so damage was minimal.

Top Sights
Natural History Museum

One of London's best-loved museums, this colossal landmark is infused with the irrepressible Victorian spirit of collecting, cataloguing and interpreting the natural world. A symphony in stone, the main museum building, designed by Alfred Waterhouse in blue and sand-coloured brick and terracotta, is as much a reason to visit as the world-famous collection within. Kids are the number one fans, but adults remain as enamoured of the exhibits as their inquisitive offspring.

◉ Map p138, C4

www.nhm.ac.uk

Cromwell Rd, SW7

admission free

⊙ 10am-5.50pm

⊖ South Kensington

Natural History Museum

Don't Miss

Architecture

Don't miss stopping to admire the astonishing architecture designed by Alfred Waterhouse: with carved pillars, animal bas-reliefs, sculptures of plants and beasts, leaded windows and sublime arches, the museum is a work of art and a labour of love.

Diplodocus Skeleton
CENTRAL HALL

It's hard to match any of the other exhibits with the initial sight of the overarching Diplodocus skeleton rising when you enter the Central Hall just ahead of the main entrance. A herbivorous quadruped, Diplodocus (double beamed lizard) was one of the longest dinosaurs, and weighed in at around 12 to 16 tons.

Dinosaur Gallery
BLUE ZONE

Children immediately yank their parents to the fantastic dinosaur gallery. With an impressive overhead walkway past twitchy-looking Velociraptors, it culminates in the museum's star attraction down the ramp: the awesome roaring and tail-flicking animatronic *T. rex*. Make your way back via hands-on exhibits on dinosaurs, including a skeleton of a triceratops (a vegetarian, despite its fearsome appearance).

Blue Whale
BLUE ZONE

Hanging from the ceiling, this life-sized mock-up of a blue whale is one of the museum's star attractions. Even bigger than the dinosaurs, the Blue Whale (*Balaenoptera musculus*) is the largest creature to have existed, weighing two tons at

☑ Top Tips

▶ Try to schedule a visit on the last Friday of the month, when the museum is open till 10pm (except December) and there is live jazz in the hall as well as special pop-up restaurants.

▶ Step-free access for disabled visitors is on Exhibition Rd.

✕ Take a Break

The museum is huge and will drain even the most seasoned museum-goer. Handily located behind the main staircase in the Central Hall, the **Central Hall Café** (⏱10am-5.30pm) serves hot and cold drinks and snacks.

The **Restaurant** (11am-5pm) in the Green Zone serves pizza, burgers, salads and has a kids' menu.

birth, while adult Blue Whales consume over four tons of krill daily!

Green Zone
The Mineral Gallery is a breathtaking display of architectural perspective leading to the Vault, where a dazzling collection includes a beautiful example of Butterscotch Crystals. The intriguing 'Treasures' exhibition in the Cadogan Gallery houses a host of unrelated objects each telling its own story, from a chunk of moon rock to a Barbary lion skull.

Creepy Crawlies
Learn the difference between millipedes and centipedes, find out how locust swarms happen, and take a closer look at spiders, crickets, ants, termites and their many multi-legged relatives. The gallery is interactivity galore, with videos, sounds and even live specimens to observe.

Earth Galleries
RED ZONE

The Earth Galleries are easily accessed from the Exhibition Rd entrance. Swapping Victorian fustiness for sleek, modern design, the black walls of the Earth Hall are lined with crystals, gems and precious rocks. By the Rio Tinto Atrium escalator, discover how the skull of a mastodon spawned the myth of the Cyclops (because of the hole in its skull where the trunk attached).

Earth's Treasury
RED ZONE

Part of the Earth Galleries, Earth's Treasury includes a magnificent collection of colourful minerals, gemstones and rocks ranging across the spectrum from opals to kryptonite-green dioptase and milky-white albite cat's eyes.

The Power Within
RED ZONE

Closed for refurbishment at the time of writing, the Power Within planned to reopen in autumn 2013. Its earthquake simulator mimics the Kobe earthquake of 1995 in which more than 6000 people perished. Explanations reveal that the Japanese once blamed earthquakes on Namazu, a vast and restless catfish trapped by a rock.

Darwin Centre
ORANGE ZONE

This vast centre focuses on taxonomy (the study of the natural world), with some 450,000 jars of pickled specimens, including an 8.6m-long giant squid called Archie, shown off during free guided tours every half hour (book in advance). The centre showcases some 28 million insects and six million plants in 'a giant cocoon'. Glass windows allow you to watch scientists at work.

Sensational Butterflies
Inside the **Sensational Butterflies** (adult/family £4.50/16; ⊙10am-5.50pm mid-Apr–mid-Sep) tunnel tent on the East

Natural History Museum

Lawn, there are swarms of what must originally have been called 'flutter-bys'.

Wildlife Garden

Home to thousands of British animal species, the beautiful **Wildlife Garden** (☉Apr-Oct) displays a range of British lowland habitats, even including a meadow with farm gates and a bee tree with a colony of honey bees. Late summer sees the arrival of Greyface Dartmoor sheep; ornithologists can look out for moorhens, wrens and finches.

Skating at the Museum

In winter months (November to January), a section by the East Lawn of the Natural History Museum is transformed into a glittering and highly popular ice rink. Our advice: book your slot well ahead (www.ticketmaster.co.uk), browse the museum and skate later.

Natural History Museum Shop

Not far from the Cromwell Rd museum entrance, the well-stocked shop has bundles of imaginative and educational toys, games, collectibles, stationery and books for young natural historians. It's open from 10am to 5.50pm.

Local Life
Shopping in Chelsea & Knightsbridge

From ever-fashionable Chelsea hub Sloane Sq to the well-groomed swirl of shoppers in Knightsbridge, you'll be rewarded with wonderful shopping opportunities, from charming bookshops through an inspiring design emporium, rare art nouveau architecture to exclusive handmade shoes. Pick up some souvenirs in London's signature department store and celebrate your smart buys with drinks in a classic British pub.

❶ **Peruse Art at the Saatchi Gallery**

A short walk up the King's Rd from Sloane Sq, the invigorating **Saatchi Gallery** (www.saatchi-gallery.co.uk; Duke of York's HQ, King's Rd, SW1; admission free; ⊙10am-6pm; ⊖Sloane Sq) is a must for art lovers. This excellent 6500-sq-metre space holds temporary exhibitions of contemporary international art and sculpture.

❷ Browse at John Sandoe Books

The perfect antidote to impersonal book superstores, this atmospheric and individual **bookshop** (www.john-sandoe.com; 10 Blacklands Tce; ⏱9.30am-6.30pm Mon-Sat, 11am-5pm Sun; ⊝Sloane Sq) is a treasure trove of literary gems and surprises. It's been in business for decades: loyal customers swear by it and the knowledgeable booksellers spill forth with well-read pointers.

❸ Check out the Conran Shop

Located within iconic art nouveau Michelin House, this splendid **design shop** (www.conranshop.co.uk; Michelin House, 81 Fulham Rd, SW3; ⏱10am-6pm Mon, Tue & Fri, to 7pm Wed & Thu, to 6.30pm Sat, noon-6pm Sun; ⊝South Kensington) constantly rewards visits with new ideas, from chic canvases of literary first editions, quirky gifts for the kids, lovely deco-style furniture, trendy minimalist wristwatches and much more.

❹ Size up a Pair of Church's Shoes

It can take up to eight weeks to make a pair of shoes from **Church's** (www.church-footwear.com; 143 Brompton Rd, SW3; ⏱10.30am-6.30pm Mon-Sat, noon-6pm Sun; ⊝Knightsbridge), so they will cost an arm and, more appropriately, a leg. But they have been lovingly produced in Northampton since 1873 with such exquisite care and precision they can last decades.

❺ Cutler & Gross

This flagship **boutique** (⏱9.30am-7pm Mon-Sat, noon-5pm Sun; ⊝Knightsbridge) sells a stunning range of glam, hand-made glasses frames and sunglasses to those who want to make a real splash. The colourful frames are hip and distinctive with classic undertones; new collections capturing a stylistic zeitgeist appear regularly. A branch for vintage frames is nearby at 7 Knightsbridge Green.

❻ Glam up at Harvey Nichols

London's temple of high fashion, **Harvey Nichols** (www.harveynichols.com; 109-125 Knightsbridge, SW1; ⏱10am-8pm Mon-Sat, 11.30am-6pm Sun; ⊝Knightsbridge) is where the well-heeled of London go to buy the latest Chloé and Balenciaga bags or stock up on make-up from the flagship hall. The store has exclusive lines and a fantastic range of luxury goods – and you might also spot a celebrity.

❼ A Beer in the Nag's Head

A gorgeously genteel early-19th-century drinking den located in a serene mews not far from bustling Knightsbridge, the **Nag's Head** (53 Kinnerton Street, SW1; ⏱11am-11pm Mon-Sat, noon-10.30pm Sun; ⊝Hyde Park Corner) has eccentric decor (think 19th-century cricket prints), traditional wood-panelled charm, a sunken bar and a no-mobile-phones rule. Quiet and relaxed, it's a great place to conclude a day's shopping.

A

Kensington Gardens Square

BAYSWATER

Bayswater 🚇

Hereford Rd

Inverness Tce

B

Leinster Tce

Craven Hill

C

Westbourne St

Lancaster Gate

D

Bayswater Rd

The Rir
North R

1

Queensway 🚇

Bayswater Rd

Kensington Palace Gardens

Kensington Gardens

3

The Broad Walk

Budge's Walk

Lancaster Walk

Round Pond

The Ring

The Serpent

2

🅿19

Kensington Church St

14

Palace Ave

4

Kensington Palace

Kensington Palace Green

Albert Memorial

7

KENSINGTON

3

Kensington High St

17

High St Kensington

St Alban's Gve

Hyde Park Gate

Queen's Gate Mews

11

Queen's Gate Tce

18

Kensington Rd

22

Prince Consort Rd

Exhibition Rd

Ennismore Gdns

Rutland Gate

Victoria Rd

Gloucester Rd

Queen's Gate

Imperial College Rd

Victoria & Albert Museum

4

Science Museum 1

East Lawn

Natural History Museum

Thurloe Pl

Thurloe St

8

Mичel
Hous

Cromwell Rd

Gloucester Rd

Queensberry Pl

Harrington Rd

South Kensington 🚇

15

Onslow Sq

Walt

SOUTH KENSINGTON

Gloucester Rd

27

Drayton Gdns

20

23

Old Brompton Rd

Fulham Rd

28

CHELSEA

Astell S

13

5

E   F   G   H

Marble Arch ⊖ 10

Marble Arch

Speaker's Corner

Duke St

Brook St

Grosvenor St

Conduit St

Regent St

North Audley St

New Bond St

Piccadilly

Park La

South Audley St

Berkeley St

ST JAMES'S

Hyde Park

Charles St

Curzon St

Hertford St

21

Piccadilly

Green Park ⊖

Serpentine Rd

Green Park

Queen's Walk

Rotten Row

Apsley House 5 ⊙

6 ⊙ Wellington Arch

Constitution Hill

The Mall

South Carriage Dr

KNIGHTSBRIDGE

Knightsbridge ⊖

Hyde Park Corner

Buckingham Palace Gardens

Birdcage Walk

Knightsbridge ⊖

Lowndes St

Buckingham Gate

12 ✖

Brompton Rd

16 ✖

Belgrave Sq

Belgrave Pl

Grosvenor Gardens

Palace St

Victoria St

26 🔒

Beauchamp Pl

Pont St

Belgrave Square

Hobart Pl

Westminster Cathedral ⊙ 9

Sloane St

Eaton Pl

Eaton Sq

Grosvenor Gardens

Buckingham Palace Rd

Victoria St

Cadogan Pl

Eaton Sq

Chester Sq

Victoria ⊖ Victoria

Vauxhall Bridge Rd

29 🔒

Sloane Tce →

25 ✪

South Eaton Pl

Elizabeth St

Victoria Coach Station (Arrivals)

Belgrave Rd

Wilton Rd

24 ✪

Eaton Tce

Victoria Coach Station

Draycott Ave

Sloane Ave

Draycott Pl

Sloane Sq ⊖

King's Rd

Lower Sloane St

Pimlico Rd

Warwick Way

PIMLICO

ystan Pl

N 0   500 m
0   0.25 miles

Sights

Science Museum MUSEUM

1 Map p138, C4

With seven floors of interactive and educational exhibits, this scientifically spellbinding museum will mesmerise even the most precocious of young know-it-alls. Some children head for the ground-floor shop's voice warpers, lava lamps, boomerangs, bouncy globes and alien babies, and stay put. Highlights include the Energy Hall on the ground floor and the riveting Flight Gallery on the 3rd. (www.sciencemuseum.org.uk; Exhibition Rd, SW7; admission free; ⏰10am-6pm; ⊖South Kensington)

Hyde Park PARK

2 Map p138, E2

London's largest royal park spreads over 142 hectares of neatly manicured gardens, wild expanses of overgrown grass and glorious trees. Hyde Park is separated from Kensington Gardens by the L-shaped Serpentine, a small lake once fed with waters from the River Westbourne; the lake hosted the Olympic triathlon and marathon swimming events in 2012. (⏰5.30am-midnight; ⊖Marble Arch, Hyde Park Corner, Queensway)

Kensington Gardens GARDENS

3 Map p138, A2

Immediately west of Hyde Park and across the Serpentine lake are these gardens, technically part of Kensington Palace. Highlights include the

Serpentine Gallery (www.serpentinegallery.org; admission free; ⏰10am-6pm; 📶; ⊖Lancaster Gate or Knightsbridge), one of London's most important contemporary art galleries, the thoughtfully conceived **Princess Diana Memorial Fountain** and George Frampton's celebrated **Peter Pan statue**, close to the lake. (⏰dawn-dusk; ⊖High St Kensington)

Take a Break Stop for afternoon tea and pastry at the Orangery (p143).

Kensington Palace PALACE

4 Map p138, B2

Built in 1605 and most recently restored in 2011, the palace became the favourite royal residence under William and Mary of Orange in 1689, and remained so until George III became king and relocated to Buckingham Palace. It still has various apartments where members of the royal family live. Highlights include **Fashion Rules**, a collection of royal dresses, and the **Cupola Room**. (www.hrp.org.uk/kensingtonpalace; Kensington Gardens, W8; adult/child £14.50/free; ⏰10am-6pm; ⊖High St Kensington)

Apsley House HISTORIC HOME

5 Map p138, F3

This stunning house was designed by Robert Adam for Baron Apsley in the late 18th century, but was later sold to the first Duke of Wellington, who lived here until his death in 1852. Wellington memorabilia fills the basement gallery, while the stairwell is dominated by Antonio Canova's stag-

Serpentine Gallery summer cafe, Kensington Gardens

gering 3.4m-high statue of a fig-leafed Napoleon. Don't miss the elaborate Portuguese silver service. (www.english-heritage.org.uk; 149 Piccadilly, W1; adult/child £6.30/3.80, with Wellington Arch £8.20/4.90; ⊘11am-5pm Wed-Sun Apr-Oct, to 4pm Wed-Sun Nov-Mar; ⊖Hyde Park Corner)

Wellington Arch   MUSEUM

6 ◉ Map p138, G3

This magnificent neoclassical 1826 arch, facing Apsley House in the green space strangled by the Hyde Park Corner roundabout, is topped by Europe's largest bronze sculpture, *Peace Descending on the Quadriga of War* (1912). Until the 1960s, part of the monument served as a tiny police station, then it was opened to

the public as a three-floor exhibition space with unforgettable views. (www.english-heritage.org.uk; Hyde Park Corner, W1; adult/child 5-15 £4/2.40, with Apsley House £8.20/4.90; ⊘10am-5pm Wed-Sun Apr-Oct, 10am-4pm Wed-Sun Nov-Mar; 🐾; ⊖Hyde Park Corner)

Albert Memorial   MONUMENT

7 ◉ Map p138, C3

This splendid Victorian confection on the southern edge of Kensington Gardens, facing the Royal Albert Hall, is as ostentatious as the subject (Queen Victoria's German husband, Albert; 1819–61) was purportedly humble. Albert explicitly insisted he did not want a monument but, ignoring the good prince's wishes, the Lord

Local Life

Speakers' Corner

The northeastern corner of Hyde Park is traditionally the spot for soapbox ranting. It's the only place in Britain where demonstrators can assemble without police permission. **Speakers' Corner** (Map p138, E1; Park Lane; ⊖Marble Arch) was frequented by Karl Marx, Vladimir Lenin, George Orwell and William Morris. If you've got something to get off your chest, do so on Sunday, although you'll mainly have fringe dwellers, religious fanatics and hecklers for company.

Mayor instructed George Gilbert Scott to build the 53m-high, gaudy Gothic memorial in 1872. (☏020-7936 2568; www.royalparks.org.uk/parks/kensington-gardens/kensington-gardens-attractions/the-albert-memorial; tours adult/concession £6/5; ⊗tours 2pm & 3pm 1st Sun of month Mar-Dec; ⊖Knightsbridge, Gloucester Rd)

Michelin House HISTORIC BUILDING

8 ◉ Map p138, D5

Built for Michelin between 1905 and 1911 by François Espinasse, and completely restored in 1985, this building blurs the stylish line between art nouveau and art deco. The iconic roly-poly Michelin Man (Bibendum) appears in the exquisite modern stained glass (the originals were removed at the outbreak of WWII and subsequently vanished), while the lobby is decorated with tiles showing

early-20th-century cars. (81 Fulham Rd, SW3; admission free; ⊖South Kensington)

Westminster Cathedral CHURCH

9 ◉ Map p138, H4

With its distinctive candy-striped red-brick and white-stone tower features, John Francis Bentley's 19th-century cathedral, the mother church of Roman Catholicism in England and Wales, is a splendid example of neo-Byzantine architecture. Although construction started in 1896 and worshippers began attending services seven years later, the church ran out of money and the gaunt interior remains largely unfinished. (www.westminstercathedral.org.uk; Victoria St, SW1; tower adult/child £5/2.50; ⊗7am-7pm; 🖥; ⊖Victoria)

Marble Arch MONUMENT

10 ◉ Map p138, E1

Designed by John Nash in 1827, this huge white arch was moved here from its original spot in front of Buckingham Palace in 1851, when adjudged too unimposing an entrance to the royal manor. If you're feeling anarchic, walk through the central portal, a privilege reserved by (unenforced) law for the Royal Family and the ceremonial King's Troop Royal Horse Artillery. (⊖Marble Arch)

Eating

Launceston Place

MODERN BRITISH ££

11 Map p138, B4

This exceptionally handsome Michelin-starred restaurant, hidden away on a picture-postcard Kensington street of Edwardian houses, is super-chic. Prepared by Yorkshire chef Tim Allen, the food is a gastronomic pleasure, and is accompanied by an award-winning wine list. The adventurous will aim for the six-course tasting menu (£65; vegetarian available). (☑020-7937 6912; www.launcestonplace-restaurant.co.uk; 1a Launceston Pl, W8; 3-course lunch/Sun lunch/dinner £25/29.50/30; ⊘closed lunch Mon; ☑; ⊖Gloucester Rd, High St Kensington)

Dinner by Heston Blumenthal

MODERN BRITISH £££

12 Map p138, E3

A sumptuously presented gastronomic tour de force, taking diners on a journey through British culinary history (with inventive modern inflections). Dishes carry dates to convey historical context, while the restaurant interior is a design triumph, from the glass-walled kitchen and its overhead clock mechanism to the large windows onto the park. (☑020-7201 3833; www.dinner-byheston.com; Mandarin Oriental Hyde Park, 66 Knightsbridge, SW1; set lunch £36, mains £26-38; ⊘noon-2.30pm & 6.30-10.30pm; ⊖Knightsbridge)

Tom's Kitchen

MODERN EUROPEAN ££

13 Map p138, D5

Celebrity chef Tom Aikens' restaurant serves excellent food, including award-winning breakfasts and pancakes. (☑020-7349 0202; www.tomskitchen.co.uk; 27 Cale St; breakfast £4-15, mains £13.90-30; ⊘8-11.30am, noon-2.30pm & 6.30-10.30pm Mon-Fri, 10am-3.30pm, 6-9.30pm Sat & Sun; ⊖South Kensington)

Orangery

TEAHOUSE ££

14 Map p138, B2

Housed in an 18th-century conservatory on the grounds of Kensington Palace, the Orangery is lovely for lunch, especially if the sun is beaming. But the standout experience here is afternoon tea. (☑020-3166 6112; www.hrp.org.uk/kensingtonpalace/foodanddrink/orangery; Kensington Palace, Kensington Gardens, W8; tea £22.65, with Champagne £32.50; ⊘10am-6pm Mar-Sep, to 5pm Oct-Feb; ⊖Queensway, Notting Hill Gate, High St Kensington)

Top Tip

Queen's Life Guard

Catch the Queen's Life Guard (Household Cavalry) departing for Horse Guards Parade at 10.32am (9.32am on Sunday) from Hyde Park Barracks for the daily Changing of the Guard, a ritual that dates to 1660. They troop via Hyde Park Corner, Constitution Hill and the Mall.

Daquise

POLISH ££

15 Map p138, D5

With an unassuming yet wholesome interior, this popular Polish restaurant welcomes diners with a heart-warming range of vodkas and a reasonably priced, regularly varying menu, where you can usually find the oft-seen *bigos*, a 'hunter's stew' of cabbage and pork, and an abundance of soups. The Monday to Saturday espresso lunch (£9) is attractively priced. (☎020-7589 6117; http://daquise.co.uk; 20 Thurloe St, SW7; mains £15-22; ☺noon-11pm; ☻South Kensington)

Zuma

JAPANESE £££

16 Map p138, E3

A modern-day take on the traditional Japanese *izakaya* ('a place to stay and drink sake'), where drinking and eating harmonise, Zuma oozes style. Traditional Japanese materials – wood and stone – combine with modern touches for a highly contemporary feel. The private *kotatsu* rooms are the place for large dinner groups, or dine alongside the sushi-counter, open-plan kitchen. (☎020-7584 1010; www.zumarestaurant.com; 5 Raphael St, SW7; mains £15-75; ☺6-11pm daily & noon-2.30pm Mon-Fri, 12.30-3.30pm Sat & Sun; ☏; ☻Knightsbridge)

Drinking

Kensington Roof Gardens

BAR, CLUB

17 Map p138, A3

Atop the former Derry and Toms building high above Kensington High St is this enchanting venue – a bar/club with 0.6 hectares of gardens. There are three different gardens: the stunningly beautiful Spanish gardens inspired by the Alhambra in Granada; the Tudor gardens, all nooks, crannies and fragrant flowers; and the Woodlands gardens, home to ancient trees and four flamingos. (www.roofgardens.virgin.com; 99 Kensington High St, W8; ☺10pm-3am Fri & Sat, May-Sep; ☻High St Kensington)

Zuma

BAR

After the hectic shopping swirl of Knightsbridge, the stylish simplicity and muted elegance of Zuma (see 16 Map p138, E3) is refreshingly soothing. As are the ambitious 40-plus varieties of sake and exquisitely presented cocktails (many blended with Japanese spirits) served to the assorted high-rollers at the bar. If your taste buds warm to the occasion, the fantastic restaurant awaits. (www.zumarestaurant.com; 5 Raphael St; ☺noon-11.30pm; ☏; ☻Knightsbridge)

Queen's Arms

PUB

18 Map p138, C4

Just around the corner from the Royal Albert Hall, this blue-grey painted pub in an adorable cobbled setting off bustling Queen's Gate beckons with a cosy interior and a right royal selection of ales and ciders on tap. (www.thequeensarmskensington.co.uk; 30 Queen's Gate Mews, SW7; ⊘noon-11pm Mon-Sat, noon-10.30pm Sun; ⊖Gloucester Rd)

Churchill Arms PUB

19 ⊕ Map p138, A2

With its cascade of geraniums and Union Jack flags swaying in the breeze, the Churchill Arms is quite a sight on Kensington Church St. Renowned for its Winston memorabilia and dozens of knick-knacks on the walls, the pub is a favourite of both locals and tourists. The attached conservatory has been serving excellent Thai food for two decades (mains £6 to £10). (www.churchillarmskensington.co.uk; 119 Kensington Church St; ⊘11am-11pm Mon-Wed, 11am-midnight Thu-Sat, noon-10.30pm Sun; 🛜; ⊖Notting Hill Gate)

Drayton Arms PUB

20 ⊕ Map p138, B5

This vast, comely Victorian corner boozer is delightful inside and out, with some bijou art-nouveau features (sinuous tendrils and curlicues above the windows and the doors), contemporary art on the walls, fabulous coffered ceiling and heated beer garden. The crowd is both hip and down-to-earth, and there's a great beer and wine selection. (www.thedraytonarmssw5.co.uk; 153 Old Brompton Rd, SW5; ⊘noon-11pm Mon-Sat, noon-10.30pm Sun; 🚌430, ⊖Gloucester Rd, South Kensington)

MIKE BOOTH/ALAMY ©

Orangery (p143)

Galvin at Windows BAR

21 ⊕ Map p138, G2

This swish bar on the edge of Hyde Park opens onto stunning views, especially at dusk. Cocktail prices reach similar heights (£11.50 to £15.25) but the leather seats are comfortable and the marble bar is gorgeous. The restaurant (same views, one Michelin star) offers a giveaway two- and three-course lunch menu for £25 and £29. (www.galvinatwindows.com; London Hilton on Park Lane, 28th fl, 22 Park Lane, W1; ⊘11am-1am Mon-Wed, to 3am Thu-Sat, to 11pm Sun; ⊖Hyde Park Corner)

Entertainment

Royal Albert Hall
CONCERT HALL

22 Map p138, C3

This splendid Victorian concert hall hosts classical-music, rock and other performances, but is most famously the venue for the BBC-sponsored Proms. Booking is possible, but from mid-July to mid-September Proms punters also queue for £5 standing (or 'promenading') tickets that go on sale one hour before curtain-up. (☑020-7589 8212; www.royalalberthall.com; Kensington Gore, SW7; ⊖South Kensington)

606 Club
BLUES, JAZZ

23 Map p138, C5

Named after its old address on King's Rd (which cast a spell over jazz lovers London-wide back in the '80s), this fantastic, tucked-away basement jazz club and restaurant gives centre stage to contemporary British-based

Top Tip

Albert Hall Tours

You can take a one-hour front-of-house **guided tour** (☑0845 401 5045; adult/concession £11.50/9.50; ⊙hourly 10am-4.30pm) of the Albert Hall from the box office at door 12. **Backstage tours** (☑0845 401 5045; adult £16) (90 minutes) are also available, but far less frequent (roughly one day a month; check website).

jazz musicians. Hidden behind a nondescript brick wall, the club frequently opens until 2am, although at weekends you have to dine to gain admission (booking is advised). (☑020-7352 5953; www.606club.co.uk; 90 Lots Rd, SW10; music fee Sun-Thu £10, Fri & Sat £12; ⊙7pm-late Mon-Thu, 8pm-late Fri & Sat, 7-11.15pm Sun; ⊖Fulham Broadway)

Royal Court Theatre
THEATRE

24 Map p138, F5

Equally renowned for staging innovative new plays and old classics, the Royal Court is among London's most progressive theatres and has continued to foster major writing talent across the UK. Tickets are £10 on Monday; tickets for under 26s are £8. Check the theatre's Facebook page for the latest on cheap tickets. (☑020-7565 5000; www.royalcourttheatre.com; Sloane Sq, SW1; ⊖Sloane Sq)

Cadogan Hall
CONCERT VENUE

25 Map p138, F5

Home of the Royal Philharmonic Orchestra, Cadogan Hall is a major venue for classical music, opera and choral music, with occasional dance, rock, jazz and family concerts. (☑020-7730 4500; www.cadoganhall.com; 5 Sloane Tce, SW1; tickets £10-40; ⊖Sloane Sq)

Shopping

Harrods
DEPARTMENT STORE

26 🔒 Map p138, E3

Both garish and stylish at the same time, perennially crowded Harrods is an obligatory stop for London's tourists, from the cash strapped to the big spenders. The stock is astonishing and you'll swoon over the food hall. (www.harrods.com; 87 Brompton Rd, SW1; ⏱10am-8m Mon-Sat, 11.30am-6pm Sun; ⊖Knightsbridge)

Slightly Foxed
BOOKS

27 🔒 Map p138, C5

Once owned by a nephew of Graham Greene and run by its namesake literary quarterly, this delightfully becalming two-floor oasis of literature has a strong lean towards secondhand titles (in good condition) plus new clothbound and hardback books. Reasonably priced 1st editions peek from the shelves, luring collectors. (www.foxedbooks.com; 123 Gloucester Rd; ⏱10am-7pm Mon-Sat, 11am-5pm Sun; ⊖Gloucester Rd)

Limelight Movie Art
FILM POSTERS

28 🔒 Map p138, D5

This spiffing poster shop is a necessary stop for collectors of vintage celluloid memorabilia, nostalgic browsers or film buffs. Ageing mods and Sting fans can swoon before *Quadrophenia* (£750), Ridley Scott purists will go wide-eyed before *Alien* (£475) while 007 aficionados can be shaken and stirred by the price tag of an original

Local Life
High Street Kensington

High St Kensington is a less-crowded, more-salubrious alternative to Oxford St, with all the high-street chains, plus trendy stores and shops, such as Miss Sixty, Urban Outfitters and Waterstone's booksellers. Snap up antiques in the many shops up Kensington Church St towards Notting Hill.

Diamonds Are Forever (£1000), or swept away by *Skyfall* (£125). (☎020-7751 5584; www.limelightmovieart.com; 313 King's Rd, SW3; ⏱11.30am-6pm Mon-Sat; ⊖Sloane Sq, South Kensington)

Selina Blow
CLOTHING

Located just near Lulu Guiness (see

29 🔒 Map p138, F4), Selina Blow stocks stylish garb for men and women, fashioned with a feel for period elegance and finished with a splash of exuberance. (www.selinablow.com; 1 Ellis St; ⏱10am-6pm Mon-Fri, 11am-6pm Sat; ⊖Sloane Sq)

Lulu Guinness
FASHION

29 🔒 Map p138, F4

Quirky, whimsical and eye-catching British designs, from small evening bags resembling bright lips to fun umbrellas and cosmetics bags. (☎020-7823 4828; www.luluguinness.com; 3 Ellis St, SW1; ⏱10am-6pm Mon-Sat; ⊖Sloane Sq)

Local Life
A Saturday in Notting Hill

Getting There

⊖ Notting Hill Gate station is on the Circle, District and Central Lines.

⊖ Ladbroke Grove station on the Hammersmith & City and Circle Lines is also useful.

A Saturday in Notting Hill sees the neighbourhood at its busiest and best. Portobello Market is full of vibrant colour and the area is stuffed with excellent restaurants, pubs, shops and cinemas, making the entire day an event that embraces market browsing, the culinary, the grain and grape and, last but not least, a chance to catch a film in a classic picture-house setting.

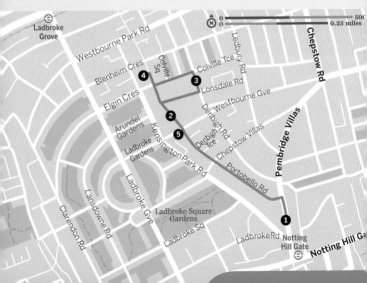

❶ Treat Yourself to an Ice Cream

A stroll in Notting Hill would not be complete without an ice cream and what better place to have one than at the lovely **Gelato Mio** (www.gelatomio.co.uk; 37 Pembridge Rd; ⊙10.30am-9pm Mon-Thu, 10.30am-10pm Fri, 9am-10pm Sat, 10am-9pm Sun; 🔊; ⊖Notting Hill Gate) ice-cream parlour, on your way to Portobello Market from Notting Hill Gate tube station.

❷ Browse the Market

Stroll along Portobello Rd until you reach the iconic **Portobello Market** (www.portobellomarket.org; Portobello Rd, W10; ⊙8am-6.30pm Mon-Wed, Fr & Sat, 8am-1pm Thu; ⊖Notting Hill Gate, Ladbroke Grove). The market mixes street food with fruit and veg, antiques, colourful fashion and trinkets.

❸ Explore a Museum

The unexpected **Museum of Brands, Packaging & Advertising** (www.museumofbrands.com; 2 Colville Mews, Lonsdale Rd, W11; adult/child £6.50/2.25; ⊙10am-6pm Tue-Sat, 11am-5pm Sun; ⊖Notting Hill Gate, Ladbroke Grove, Westbourne Park) is fairly low-tech, but eye-catching with its sponsored displays at the end of the gallery showing the evolution of packaging of well-known products, such as Johnson's Baby Powder and Guinness.

❹ Catch a Film (& a Hot Dog)

Over 100 years old, the one-of-a-kind **Electric Cinema** (☎020-7908 9696; www.electriccinema.co.uk; 191 Portobello Rd, W11; tickets £8-18; ⊖Ladbroke Grove) is the UK's oldest cinema, updated with luxurious leather armchairs and footstools. Check out what's on the program; there's mainstream, art house, classics and epic all-nighters. And when the credits start rolling, head to the excellent **Electric Diner** (www.electricdiner.com; 191 Portobello Rd; mains from £7; ⊙8am-midnight Mon-Thu, 8am-1am Fri-Sun) next door for top-notch hot dogs.

❺ Drinks at the Earl of Lonsdale

The **Earl of Lonsdale** (277-281 Portobello Rd, W11; ⊙noon-11pm Mon-Sat, noon-10.30pm Sun; ⊖Notting Hill Gate, Ladbroke Grove) is peaceful during the day, with a mixture of old biddies and young hipsters inhabiting its charming snugs. There are Samuel Smith's ales, and a fantastic backroom with sofas, banquettes and open fires, as well as a fine beer garden shaded by a towering tree of whopping girth.

Notting Hill Carnival

If you visit in late August, don't miss the carnival. Launched in 1964 by the local Afro-Caribbean community keen to celebrate its culture and traditions, **Notting Hill Carnival** (www.thenottinghillcarnival.com) has become Europe's largest street festival (up to one million people). Musical processions finish around 9pm, although parties in bars, restaurants and seemingly every house in the neighbourhood go on late into the night. There are dozens of Caribbean food stands, and celebrity chefs often make an appearance, too.

Explore

Regent's Park & Camden

Regent's Park, Camden Market and Hampstead Heath should top your list for excursions into North London. Camden is a major sight with an intoxicating energy and brilliant nightlife, while Regent's Park is an oasis of calm and sophistication amidst the North London buzz. Meanwhile, Hampstead Heath offers you a glorious day out and an insight into how North Londoners spend their weekend.

The Sights in a Day

🌅 Start your exploration with a morning trip to **Regent's Park** (p154) and the outstanding **London Zoo** (p154). For a leisurely and picturesque 20-minute stroll to Camden, walk alongside **Regent's Canal** (p154) on the north side of Regent's Park, taking in **Primrose Hill** (p154) and its gorgeous park en route. In Camden Town, lunch at **Market** (p155) for top-notch Modern British food or nibble your way around an eclectic variety of snacks at **Camden Market** (p159).

🔆 Further explore the markets before rewarding yourself with a delectable ice cream from **Chin Chin Labs** (p155) or by sitting in the beer garden of the **Edinboro Castle** (p156) for an afternoon drink.

🌙 For dinner, try the Caribbean delights at **Mango Room** (p156). The rest of the night is easily sewn up: Camden has some tremendous pubs and a glut of live music options embracing most musical persuasions, so night owls will find little reason to leave. Try jazz at **Blues Kitchen** (p157) or indie rock at **Barfly** (p157).

For a local's day on Hampstead Heath, see p160.

 Best of London

Drinking & Nightlife

Edinboro Castle (p156)

Lock Tavern (p156)

Parks & Gardens

Hampstead Heath (p160)

Regent's Park (p154)

For Kids

London Zoo (p154)

Chin Chin Labs (p155)

Getting There

🚇 **Tube** For Regent's Park, Baker St (on the Jubilee, Metropolitan, Circle, Hammersmith & City and Bakerloo Lines) is most useful.

🚇 **Tube** Useful stations for Camden are Camden Town and Chalk Farm on the Northern Line. Hampstead is also on the Northern Line.

A
B
C
D
E
1
2
3
4
0
500 m
0
0.25 miles
KENTISH TOWN
CAMDEN
PRIMROSE HILL
BELSIZE PARK
Kentish Town Rd
Gaisford St
Patshull Rd
Lawford Rd
Rochester Rd
Rochester Pl
Wilmot Pl
St Pancras Way
Camden Rd
Camden St
Greenland Rd
Bayham St
Pratt St
Angler's La
Castle Rd
Lewis St
Hawley Rd
Camden Market
Kentish Town West
Hadley St
Hartland Rd
Jamestown Rd
Camden Town
Parkway
Inverness St
Oval Rd
Gloucester Ave
Regent's Canal
Spring Pl
Grafton Rd
Athlone St
Wilkin St
Harmood St
Chalk Farm Rd
Ferdinand St
Rhyl St
Marsden St
Prince of Wales Rd
Crogsland Rd
Malden Rd
Queen's Cres
Chalk Farm
Albert Rd
Chalcot Rd
Regent's Park Rd
Fitzroy Rd
Primrose Hill
Erskine Rd
Maitland Park
Maitland Park Villas Rd
Eton College Rd
Adelaide Rd
Eton Villas
Eton Rd
Haverstock Hill
King Henry's Rd
Ainger Rd
England's La
Antrim Rd
Primrose Gardens
Belsize Park
Belsize Gve
Elsworthy Rise
Elsworthy Rd
Lambolle Pl
Belsize Park Gardens
Lamboll e Rd
Lancaster Gve
Eton Ave
Fellows Rd
Wadham Gdns
Belsize Ave
Ave Rd
1
3
5
6
8
9
11
12
13
14
15
16
17
18
19
20
21
22

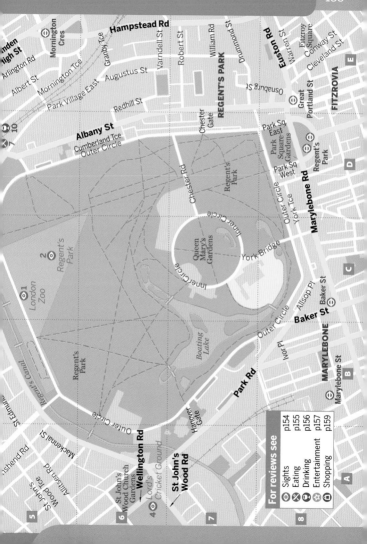

Hampstead Rd

nden
igh St

Mornington
Cres

Arlington Rd

Albert St

Mornington Tce

Park Village East · Augustus St

Granby Tce

Varndell St

Robert St

William Rd

Drummond St

Euston Rd

Warren St

Fitzroy
Square

Conway St

Cleveland St

Redhill St

REGENT'S PARK

Ossulston St

**Great
Portland St**

FITZROVIA

Albany St
Cumberland Tce
Outer Circle

Chester
Gate

Chester Rd

Park Sq
East

Park
Square
Gardens

Park Sq
West

Regent's
Park

D

Regent's
Park

Outer Circle

York Tce

Marylebone Rd

Inner Circle

Queen
Mary's
Gardens

York Bridge

Allsop Pl

Baker St

Baker St

C

2
Regent's
Park

1
London
Zoo

Regent's Canal

Regent's
Park

Boating
Lake

Outer Circle

Ivor Pl

Marylebone St

MARYLEBONE

B

Marylebone St

nburn Rd

Mackennal St

Outer Circle

Hanover
Gate

Park Rd

hend Rd

St John's
Wood Tce

Allitsen Rd

St John's
Wood Church
Gardens

4
Lord's
Cricket Ground

Wellington Rd

**St John's
Wood Rd**

A

5

6

7

8

For reviews see	
⊙ Sights	p154
⊗ Eating	p155
⍭ Drinking	p156
✪ Entertainment	p157
⊜ Shopping	p159

Sights

London Zoo
ZOO

1 ◉ Map p152, C5

These famous zoological gardens have come a long way since being established in 1828, with massive investments making conservation, education and breeding the name of the game. Highlights include Tiger Territory, Penguin Beach, Gorilla Kingdom and Butterfly Paradise. Feeding sessions or talks take place during the day. (www.londonzoo.co.uk; Outer Circle, Regent's Park, NW1; adult/child £25/19; ⏱10am-5.30pm Mar-Oct, to 4pm Nov-Feb; ⊖Camden Town)

Local Life
Walking along Regent's Canal

The canals that were once a trade lifeline for the capital have become a favourite escape for Londoners, providing a quiet walk away from traffic and crowds. You can walk along **Regent's Canal** from Little Venice to Camden in under an hour; you'll pass Regent's Park, London Zoo, Primrose Hill, beautiful villas designed by architect John Nash as well as old industrial buildings redeveloped into trendy blocks of flats. Allow 15 to 20 minutes between Camden and Regent's Park, and 25 to 30 minutes between Regent's Park and Little Venice. There are plenty of exits and signposts along the way.

Regent's Park
PARK

2 ◉ Map p152, C5

The most elaborate and ordered of London's many parks, this one was created around 1820 by John Nash, who planned to use it as an estate to build palaces for the aristocracy. Although the plan never quite came off, you can get some idea of what Nash might have achieved from the buildings along the Outer Circle. (www.royalparks.org.uk; ⏱5am-dusk; ⊖Regent's Park, Baker St)

Primrose Hill
NEIGHBOURHOOD

3 ◉ Map p152, C3

Wedged between well-heeled Regent's Park and edgy Camden, the little neighbourhood of Primrose Hill is high on the wish list of most Londoners – but utterly unaffordable. With its independent boutiques, lovely restaurants and good pubs, it has a rare village feel. The proximity of the gorgeous, eponymous park, with fabulous views of London, is another draw. (⊖Chalk Farm, Camden Town)

Lord's Cricket Ground
CRICKET GROUND

4 ◉ Map p152, A6

The 'home of cricket' is a must for any devotee of this peculiarly English game: book early for the test matches, but cricket buffs should also take the absorbing and anecdotal 90-minute tour of the ground and facilities. (www.lords.org; St John's Wood Rd, NW8; tours adult/child £15/9; ⏱tours 11am, noon & 2pm Mon-Fri, 10am & 1pm Sat & Sun; ⊖St John's Wood)

Eating

Market

MODERN BRITISH **££**

  Map p152, D4

This fabulous restaurant is an ode to great, simple British food with a hint of European thrown in. The light and airy space with bare brick walls, steel tables and basic wooden chairs reflects this simplicity. The menu's delights include roast poussin with baby spring vegetables, and whole plaice with caper butter and chips. (☏020-7267 9700; www.marketrestaurant. co.uk; 43 Parkway, NW1; 2-course lunch £10, mains £10-14; ☺noon-2.30pm & 6-10.30pm Mon-Sat, 1-3.30pm Sun; ⊖Camden Town)

Chin Chin Labs

ICE CREAM **£**

Map p152, D3

This is food chemistry at its best: say hello to liquid nitrogen ice cream. Each is custom-made (chefs prepare the base and freeze it on the spot by adding liquid nitrogen). Flavours change regularly and match the seasons (spiced hot cross bun, mango brûlée); sauces and toppings are equally creative. (www.chinchinlabs.com; 49-50 Camden Lock Pl, NW1; from £3.95; ☺noon-7pm Tue-Sun; ⊖Camden Town, Chalk Farm)

York & Albany

BRASSERIE **££**

Map p152, D5

This brasserie, part of Gordon Ramsay's empire, serves classics with a Mediterranean twist, such as roast leg

Market

of rabbit with potatoes and anchovies. The food is pitch-perfect and the setting informal; you can eat at the bar, lounge or more formal dining room. (www.gordonramsay.com/yorkandalbany; 127-129 Parkway, NW1; mains £14-24, 2-/3-course menu £19/22; ☺7-11am, noon-3pm & 6-11pm Mon-Sat, 7am-9pm Sun; ⍓; ⊖Camden Town)

Manna

VEGETARIAN **££**

Map p152, B3

Tucked away on a side street in Primrose Hill, this little place does a brisk trade in inventive vegetarian cooking. The menu features dishes such as green korma, wild garlic and pea risotto cake, and superb desserts. There are excellent vegan options and everything comes beautifully presented, from

Local Life

Taste of London

Not content with having some very fine restaurants, Londoners love their food festivals too. Having celebrated its 10th edition in 2013, **Taste of London** (www.tastefestivals. com/london; Regent's Park, NW1; ⊙ Jun) is now one of the most well-established. It turns Regent's Park into a haze of Michelin stars, with top chefs rivalling each other for festival-goers' attention.

fan-shaped salads to pyramidal mains. Reservations are usually essential. (☎020-7722 8082; www.mannav.com; 4 Erskine Rd, NW3; mains £14-20; ⊙6.30-10.30pm Tue-Fri, noon-3pm & 6.30-10.30pm Sat, noon-3pm Sun; ☑; ☉Chalk Farm)

Mango Room

 CARIBBEAN ££

9 Map p152, E4

With its modern, bright decor and excellent service, Mango Room promises a sophisticated Caribbean experience, with food to match: grilled sea bass with coconut milk and sweet pepper sauce, salt fish with *ackee* (a yellow-skinned Jamaican fruit that has an uncanny resemblance to scrambled eggs), and curried goat with hot pepper and spices, all presented with origami intricacy. Booking recommended. (☎020-7482 5065; www.mangoroom.co.uk; 10-12 Kentish Town Rd, NW1; mains £12-15; ⊙noon-midnight; ☉Camden Town)

Drinking

Edinboro Castle

PUB

10 Map p152, D5

A reliable Camden boozer, the large and relaxed Edinboro has a refined Primrose Hill atmosphere. It boasts a full menu, gorgeous furniture designed for slumping and a fine bar. Where the pub comes into its own is in its huge beer garden, complete with BBQ and table football and adorned with fairy lights for long summer evenings. (www.edinborocastlepub.co.uk; 57 Mornington Tce, NW1; ⊙noon-11pm; ☎; ☉Camden Town)

Lock Tavern

PUB

11 Map p152, D3

An institution in Camden, the Lock Tavern rocks for several reasons: it's cosy inside, has a roof terrace from where you can watch the market throngs, the food is good, the beer plentiful and it has a roll-call of guest bands and DJs at the weekend to spice things up. (www.lock-tavern.co.uk; 35 Chalk Farm Rd, NW1; ⊙noon-midnight Mon-Thu, to 1am Fri & Sat, to 11pm Sun; ☉Chalk Farm)

Black Cap

GAY

12 Map p152, E4

This friendly place is Camden's premier gay venue, and attracts people from all over North London. There's an outdoor terrace, the pub-like upstairs Shufflewick bar and the downstairs club, where you'll find hilarious camp cabaret as well as decent dance music. (www.theblackcap.com; 171 Camden High St, NW1; ⊘noon-1am Sun-Tue, to 2am Wed & Thu, to 3am Fri & Sat; ⊖Camden Town)

Queen's   PUB

13 🍺 Map p152, B4

Perhaps because this is Primrose Hill, the interior is more cafe than pub. Still, it's a good one, with a nice wine list, ales and lagers and, more importantly, plenty of people-watching to do with your pint; Jude Law and many of Primrose Hill's fashionistas come here for a tipple. (www.thequeensprimrosehill.co.uk; 49 Regent's Park Rd, NW1; ⊘11am-11pm Mon-Sat, noon-10.30pm; 🛜🚹; ⊖Chalk Farm)

Entertainment

Blues Kitchen   LIVE MUSIC

14 ⭐ Map p152, E4

The Blues Kitchen's recipe for success is simple: select brilliant blues bands, host them in a fabulous bar, make it (mostly) free and offer excellent food and drink. There are bands every night at 10pm and jamming sessions at 7.30pm on Sundays. Usually free before 10pm. (www.theblueskitchen.com; 111-113 Camden High St, NW1; free-£6; ⊘noon-midnight Mon & Tue, to 1am Wed, Thu & Sun, to 3am Fri & Sat; ⊖Camden Town)

Proud Camden   LIVE MUSIC

15 ⭐ Map p152, D3

Camden's former Horse Hospital, which looked after horses injured pulling barges on nearby Grand Union Canal, is now one of Camden's great music venues. There are live bands, DJs and art exhibitions. It's fantastic in summer, when the terrace is open. The old stables are now drinking booths (although we're not sure about the recent addition of dancing poles). (www.proudcamden.com; Horse Hospital, Stables Market, NW1; free-£15; ⊘11am-1.30am Wed, to 2.30am Thu-Sat; ⊖Camden Town, Chalk Farm)

Barfly   PUB

16 ⭐ Map p152, D3

This grungy, indie-rock venue in Camden is well known for hosting small-time artists that are looking for their big break. It's small, so you'll feel like the band is playing for you and your mates. (www.mamacolive.com/thebarfly; 49 Chalk Farm Rd, NW1; gigs from £8, club nights £3-5; ⊘7pm-3am Mon-Sat, to midnight Sun; ⊖Chalk Farm)

Local Life

North London Sounds

North London is the home of indie rock and many a famous band started playing in this area's grungy bars, including Stereophonics, Coldplay, Amy Winehouse and Feeder. Doors generally open around 7.30pm but bands may not come on until 9pm, sometimes later. Closing time is around 2am, although this can vary by event.

Edinboro Castle (p156)

Bull & Gate

LIVE MUSIC

17 ⭐ Map p152, E1

The best place to see unsigned but promising talent, this legendary old-school music venue pulls in the punters eager to see bands that might just turn out to be the next big thing. Just so you know, Coldplay, Keane, Maximo Park and Bloc Party were all spotted by the club's promoter (Club Fandango). (www.bullandgate.co.uk; 389 Kentish Town Rd, NW5; admission £6; ⏰ noon-11pm, gigs 8pm Tue-Sat; ⊖ Kentish Town)

Jazz Café

LIVE MUSIC

18 ⭐ Map p152, E4

This club's speciality is the crossover of jazz into the mainstream. It's a trendy restaurant with jazz gigs once a week, while the rest of the month is filled with Afro, funk, hip-hop, R&B and soul with big-name acts and a bohemian Camden crowd. (www.mamacolive.com/thejazzcafe; 5 Parkway, NW1; gigs from £8; club nights £5; ⏰ 7pm-2am; ⊖ Camden Town)

 Top Tip

Camden Market Snacks

There are dozens of food stalls at the Lock Market (p159) and Stables Market (p159) – virtually every type of cuisine, from French to Argentinian, Japanese and Caribbean. Quality varies but is generally pretty good and affordable, and you can eat on the big communal tables or by the canal.

Shopping

Stables Market
MARKET

19 Map p152, D3

Just beyond the railway arches, opposite Hartland Rd, the Stables is the best part of Camden Market, with antiques, Asian artefacts, rugs and carpets, pine furniture and vintage clothing. (Chalk Farm Rd, NW1; ⊗10am-6pm; ⊖Chalk Farm)

Camden Lock Market
MARKET

20 Map p152, D3

The original market, right next to the lock, with diverse food, ceramics, furniture, oriental rugs, musical instruments and designer clothes. (www.camdenlockmarket.com; 54-56 Camden Lock Pl, NW1; ⊗10am-6pm; ⊖Camden Town, Chalk Farm)

Canal Market
MARKET

21 Map p152, D3

Just over the canal bridge, Canal Market has bric-a-brac from around the world; we love the scooter seats by the

 Local Life

Camden Market

Although – or perhaps because – it stopped being cutting-edge several thousand cheap leather jackets ago, **Camden Market** (Camden High St, NW1; ⊗10am-6pm; ⊖Camden Town, Chalk Farm) gets a whopping 10 million visitors annually. Expect clothes (of variable quality), bags, jewellery, arts and crafts, candles, incense and decorative titbits. Camden Market comprises Stables Market, Lock Market, Canal Market and Buck Street Market.

canal. (Chalk Farm Rd, cnr Castlehaven Rd, NW1; ⊗10am-6pm Thu-Sun; ⊖Chalk Farm, Camden Town)

Buck Street Market
MARKET

22 Map p152, E4

This covered market sells clothing, jewellery and tourist tat. It's the closest to the station but the least interesting. (Camden High St, cnr Buck St, NW1; ⊗9am-5.30pm Thu-Sun; ⊖Camden Town)

Local Life
Walking on Hampstead Heath

Getting There

For Highgate Cem-
etery: Archway station
(Northern Line). Hamp-
stead station is also on
the Northern Line.

Hampstead Heath
and Gospel Oak
(Overground) are at
the southern end of
the heath.

Sprawling Hampstead Heath, with its rolling woodlands and meadows, feels a million miles away –
despite being approximately four – from the City
of London. Covering 320 hectares, it's home to
about 180 bird species, 23 species of butterflies,
grass snakes, bats, a rich array of flora and expansive views from the top of Parliament Hill.

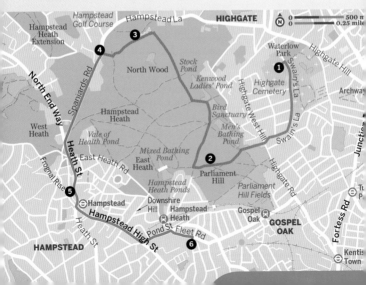

❶ Explore the Local Cemetery

The final resting place of Karl Marx, George Eliot and Russian secret service agent Alexander Litvinenko (the latter poisoned with radioactive polonium-210), **Highgate Cemetery** (www.highgatecemetery.org; Swain's Lane, N6; East Cemetery adult/child £4/free; 10am-5pm Mon-Fri, from 11am Sat & Sun; Archway) is divided into East and West. To visit the atmospheric West Cemetery, you must take a tour.

❷ Views from Parliament Hill

From the cemetery head down Swain's Lane to the roundabout with Highgate West Hill and climb to **Parliament Hill** for all-inclusive views south over town. Londoners adore picnicking here – choose your spot, tuck into some sandwiches and feast on the superb vistas. Afterwards, dip a toe in the Men's Bathing Pond or Kenwood Ladies' Pond (open all year round, lifeguard-supervised).

❸ Visit Kenwood House

Traverse the heath to the magnificent neoclassical 18th-century **Kenwood House** (www.english-heritage.org.uk; Hampstead Lane, NW3; Gospel Oak, Hampstead Heath) in a glorious sweep of perfectly landscaped gardens leading down to a picturesque lake, the setting for summer concerts. The house contains a magnificent collection of art, including paintings by Rembrandt, Constable, Turner and others.

❹ Rest at the Spaniard's Inn

At the edge of the heath is this marvellous 1585 tavern, where Byron, Shelley, Keats and Dickens all paused for a tipple. Once a toll house, the **Spaniard's Inn** (www.thespaniardshampstead.co.uk; Spaniards Rd, NW3; noon-11pm Mon-Fri, from 9am Sat, from 11am Sun; 21) has kept its historic charm – wood panelling, jumbled interior and hearty welcome – and is hugely popular with local dog walkers, families and other park revellers on weekends.

❺ Mooch Around Hampstead

After a restorative pint at the Spaniard's Inn, take bus 603 to the historic neighbourhood of **Hampstead** and mooch around this corner of London. Beloved of artists in the interwar years, it has retained a bohemian feel, with sumptuous houses, leafy streets, cafes and boutiques. Try **Exclusivo** (2 Flask Walk, NW3; 11.30am-6pm Mon-Fri, noon-6pm Sat & Sun) for top-quality, secondhand designer garments.

❻ Dinner at the Stag

Finish your day with an evening stroll down to the **Stag** (020-7722 2646; www.thestaghampstead.com; 67 Fleet Rd, NW3; mains £9.50-15; noon-11pm Mon-Thu, noon-midnight Fri & Sat, noon-10.30pm Sun; Hampstead Heath), a fine gastropub where you'll be rewarded with delicious British fare. The beef and ale pie is one of a kind and the desserts are stellar. The wine and beer selection will also ensure you're in no rush to go home.

Explore

The Royal Observatory & Greenwich

Quaint Greenwich (*gren*-itch) by the Thames in South London is packed with grand architecture, and its parks and sights draw fleets of visitors. With the Royal Observatory and the National Maritime Museum, Greenwich should be a highlight of any visit to London, so allow a day to do it justice.

The Sights in a Day

☼ Arrive early for a morning stroll around **Greenwich Park** (p167) and climb uphill for the delicious views of Greenwich and London from the statue of General Wolfe. Explore the **Royal Observatory** (p164) before heading downhill to admire the dazzling artwork in the Painted Hall of the **Old Royal Naval College** (p168).

☼ Restore some calories at **Greenwich Market** (p169) or the **Old Brewery** (p169) before heading over to the brilliant **Cutty Sark** (p167) for a voyage back to the glory days of the tea trade. Finally, make sure you spare an hour or two for the **National Maritime Museum** (p167), the world's largest of its kind, and just as riveting for adults as for children.

☽ To recover from all this sightseeing, sink a couple of drinks in one of the riverside pubs, the **Trafalgar Tavern** (p169) or the **Cutty Sark Tavern** (p169). Dine at **Inside** (p168) for modern European fare or the beautiful **Spread Eagle** (p169) for old-world interiors and French cuisine.

👁 Top Sights

Royal Observatory (p164)

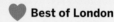 Best of London

Drinking & Nightlife
Trafalgar Tavern (p169)

Cutty Sark Tavern (p169)

Greenwich Union (p170)

Architecture
Queen's House (p167)

Old Royal Naval College (p168)

Hidden Sights
Fan Museum (p168)

Greenwich Foot Tunnel (p167)

Getting There

🚆 **Train** The quickest way from central London is via one of the mainline trains from Charing Cross or London Bridge to Greenwich station.

DLR Most sights in Greenwich can be easily reached from the Cutty Sark DLR (Docklands Light Railway) station.

⚓ **Boat** Thames Clipper boats run to Greenwich and Woolwich Arsenal from London Eye Millennium Pier.

Top Sights
Royal Observatory

Perched at the top of Greenwich Park, the Royal Observatory is where the study of the sea and the stars converge. Visitors will discover how royal astronomers managed to solve the riddle of longitude and how Greenwich became the centre of the world with Greenwich Mean Time – the meridian is right in the courtyard.

◉ Map p166, C4

www.rmg.co.uk

Greenwich Park, SE10

adult/child £7/2.50

🕙 10am-5pm

🚇 DLR Cutty Sark

Royal Observatory

Don't Miss

Flamsteed House

The original observatory building, Flamsteed House contains the magnificent Octagon Room, and the rather simple apartment where the Astronomer Royal and his family lived. Below is a series of brilliant galleries explaining how the longitude problem – how to accurately determine a ship's east–west location – was solved through astronomical means and the invention of the chronometer.

Meridian Courtyard

Outside Flamsteed House, the globe is decisively sliced into east and west by the Prime Meridian. Visitors can delightfully straddle both hemispheres in the Meridian Courtyard, with one foot either side of the meridian. Every day at 1pm the red time-ball at the top of the Royal Observatory drops, as it has done since 1833.

Astronomy Centre

The southern half of the observatory contains the highly informative Astronomy Centre, where you can touch the oldest object you will ever encounter: part of the Gibeon meteorite, a mere 4.5 billion years old! Other engaging exhibits include astronomical documentaries, a 1st edition of Newton's *Principia Mathematica* and the opportunity to view the Milky Way in multiple wavelengths.

Planetarium

The state-of-the-art **Peter Harrison Planetarium** (adult/child £6.50/4.50), London's sole planetarium, can cast entire heavens onto the inside of its roof. It runs several informative shows each day.

☑ Top Tips

▶ Access to the Royal Observatory and Planetarium are subject to admission fees but the Astronomy Centre is free.

▶ Combined tickets for the Royal Observatory, Cutty Sark and special exhibitions at the Maritime Museum offer good discounts.

▶ Being on a bluff in Greenwich Park, the Observatory offers fantastic views of London, the River Thames and the business district of Canary Wharf.

✗ Take a Break

The **Astronomy Café**, located next to the Planetarium, serves refreshments and light meals. It has access to the Gagarin Terrace, which features a statue of the celebrated cosmonaut.

If you fancy a locally brewed beer (and some lovely food), head to the Old Brewery (p170) in the grounds of the Old Royal Naval College.

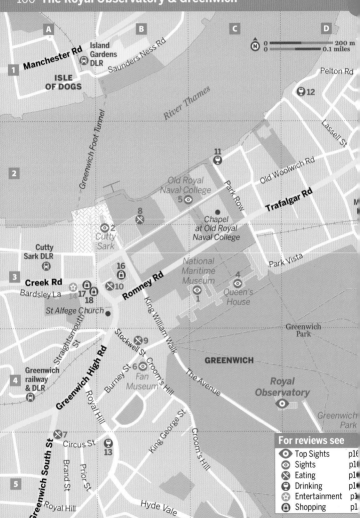

A B C D

Manchester Rd

Island Gardens DLR

ISLE OF DOGS

Saunders Ness Rd

Pelton Rd

12

River Thames

Lassell St

Greenwich Foot Tunnel

11

Old Royal Naval College

Old Woolwich Rd

5

Park Row

Trafalgar Rd

8

Chapel at Old Royal Naval College

2 Cutty Sark

Cutty Sark DLR

National Maritime Museum

Park Vista

16

4

10

Romney Rd

1

Queen's House

Creek Rd

Bardsley La

14 17 18

St Alfege Church

Greenwich Park

King William Walk

Straightsmouth St

9

Stockwell St

GREENWICH

Greenwich railway & DLR

Greenwich High Rd

Burney St

6

Croom's Hill

The Avenue

Royal Observatory

Fan Museum

Royal Hill

Greenwich Park

7

Circus St

13

Greenwich South St

Brand St

Prior St

King George St

Croom's Hill

Royal Hill

Hyde Vale

For reviews see	
◉ Top Sights	p1
◎ Sights	p1
✕ Eating	p1
☺ Drinking	p1
☆ Entertainment	p1
🔒 Shopping	p1

Sights

National Maritime Museum
MUSEUM

1 Map p166, C3

The world's largest maritime museum narrates the dramatic history of Britain as a seafaring nation. Arranged thematically, exhibits include the 19m-long golden state barge built in 1732 for Frederick, Prince of Wales, the coat that Admiral Nelson wore when he died, and a huge ship's propeller on level 1. Museum tours run at noon, 1pm and 3pm. (www.rmg.co.uk/national-maritime-museum; Romney Rd, SE10; admission free; ⏲10am-5pm; ☒DLR Cutty Sark)

Take a Break Pop over to Greenwich Market (p169) for some tasty street food.

Cutty Sark
SHIP

2 Map p166, B3

This Greenwich landmark, the last of the great clipper ships to sail between China and England in the 19th century, finally reopened in April 2012 after six years and £25 million of extensive renovations. The exhibition in the ship's hold tells her story as a tea clipper at the end of the 19th century. (www.cuttysark.org.uk; King William Walk, SE10; adult/child £12/6.50; ⏲10am-5pm; ☒DLR Cutty Sark)

Greenwich Park
PARK

3 Map p166, D4

Handsome venue of the 2012 Olympic equestrian events, this park is one of London's loveliest expanses of green, with a rose garden, picturesque walks and astonishing views from the crown of the hill near the statue of General Wolfe, opposite the Royal Observatory. In October, look out for edible chestnuts on the ground. (www.royalparks.gov. uk; King George St, SE10; ⏲6am-6pm winter, 6am-8pm spring & autumn, 6am-9pm summer; ☒Greenwich, Maze Hill, DLR Cutty Sark)

Queen's House
HISTORIC BUILDING

4 Map p166, C3

The first Palladian building by architect Inigo Jones after his return from Italy is far more enticing than the art collection it contains, even though there are Turners, Holbeins, Hogarths and Gainsboroughs. The ceremonial Great Hall is the principal room – a

Local Life
Greenwich Foot Tunnel

Greenwich is connected to the Isle of Dogs on the northern bank of the river by a cunning foot tunnel. Reached via glass-topped domes on either side of the river, the historic 370m-long **tunnel** (Cutty Sark Gardens, SE10; ⏲24 hr; ☒DLR Cutty Sark) has been in use since 1902. There are lifts and stairs on both sides.

gorgeous cube with an elaborately tiled floor dating to 1637. (www.rmg.co.uk/queens-house; Romney Rd, SE10; admission free; ⏱10am-5pm; 🚊DLR Cutty Sark)

Old Royal Naval College
HISTORIC BUILDING

5 ◉ Map p166, B2

Now used mainly by the University of Greenwich, the former Naval College is another grand undertaking from Sir Christopher Wren (of St Paul's Cathedral). The highlights are the **chapel** – decorated in a highly elaborate rococo style – and the **Painted Hall**, with its stunning baroque murals by Sir James Thornhill. (www.oldroyalnavalcollege.org; 2 Cutty Sark Gardens, SE10; admission free; ⏱10am-5pm; 🚊DLR Cutty Sark)

Fan Museum
MUSEUM

6 ◉ Map p166, B4

The world's only museum devoted entirely to fans has a wonderful collection of ivory, tortoiseshell, peacock-feather and folded-fabric examples alongside kitsch battery-powered versions and huge ornamental Welsh fans. The setting, an 18th-century Georgian town house, also has a Japanese-style garden plus the **Orangery** (half/full tea £5/6; ⏱3-5pm Tue & Sun), with lovely trompe l'œil murals and twice-weekly afternoon tea. (www.fan-museum.org; 12 Crooms Hill, SE10; adult/child £4/free; ⏱11am-5pm Tue-Sat, noon-5pm Sun; 🚊Greenwich, DLR Cutty Sark)

Eating

Inside
MODERN EUROPEAN **££**

7 ✗ Map p166, A5

With white walls, modern art and linen tablecloths, Inside is a relaxed kind of place and one of Greenwich's best restaurant offerings. The fine food hits the mark, ranging tastily and affordably from pumpkin and red lentil soup, to pan fried wild sea bass, and apple and rhubarb crumble. (✆020-8265 5060; www.insiderestaurant.co.uk; 19 Greenwich South St, SE10; mains £13.95-21.95, 2-/3-course set menu £19.95/24.95; ⏱noon-2.30pm & 6.30-10.30pm Tue-Sat, noon-3.30pm Sun; 🚊DLR Greenwich)

Old Brewery

MODERN BRITISH ££

8 Map p166, B2

A working brewery with splendidly burnished 1000L copper vats at one end and a high ceiling lit with natural sunlight, the Old Brewery is also a cafe serving lovely bistro fare by day and a restaurant by night, with a choice selection of fine dishes carefully sourced from their best seasonal ingredients. (www.oldbrewerygreenwich.com; Pepys Bldg, Old Royal Naval College, SE10; mains cafe £7-12, restaurant £10.50-18.50; ⊙cafe 10am-5pm, restaurant 6-11pm; 🚻; 🚆DLR Cutty Sark)

Spread Eagle

FRENCH £££

9 Map p166, B4

Smart, French-inspired restaurant opposite the Greenwich Theatre in what was once the terminus for the coach service to/from London. (www.spreadeaglerestaurant.co.uk; 1-2 Stockwell St, SE10; mains £12-24, lunch/dinner 2-course set-menu £13.50/22.50; ⊙noon-3pm & 6-10pm Tue-Sat, noon-5pm Sun; 🚆DLR Cutty Sark)

Tai Won Mein

CHINESE £

10 Map p166, B3

The staff here may be a little bit jaded but this great snack spot – the Cantonese moniker means 'Big Bowl of Noodles' – serves epic portions of carbohydrate-rich noodles to those overcoming Greenwich's titanic sights. (39 Greenwich Church St, SE10; mains from £4.95; ⊙11.30am-11.30pm; ✏; 🚆DLR Cutty Sark)

Drinking

Trafalgar Tavern

PUB

11 Map p166, C2

Lapped by the brown waters of the Thames, this elegant tavern with big windows looking onto the river is steeped in history. Dickens apparently knocked back a few here – and used it as the setting for the wedding breakfast scene in *Our Mutual Friend* – and prime ministers Gladstone and Disraeli used to dine on the pub's celebrated whitebait. (www.trafalgartavern.co.uk; 6 Park Row, SE10; ⊙noon-11pm Mon-Thu, to midnight Fri & Sat, to 10.30pm Sun; 🚆DLR Cutty Sark)

Cutty Sark Tavern

PUB

12 Map p166, D1

Housed in a delightful bow-windowed, wood-beamed Georgian building

Local Life
World Food at the Market

Perfect for snacking your way through a world atlas of food, **Greenwich Market** (www.shopgreenwich.co.uk/greenwich-market; College Approach, SE10; ⊙10am-5.30pm Tue-Sun; ✏; 🚆DLR Cutty Sark) is the go-to destination for anything from tapas to Thai, sushi, Polish doughnuts, crêpes, Brazilian churros, smoked Louisiana sausages, chivitos and more. Wash it all down with a glass of fresh farmhouse cider or a cup of mulled wine.

Top Tip

Free Recitals

The **Trinity Laban Conservatoire of Music & Dance** (www.trinitylaban.ac.uk) offers regular free concerts in Greenwich: they're held in St Alfege Church at 1.10pm on Thursdays and at various times in the chapel of the Old Royal Naval College (p168). Check the website for details.

directly on the Thames, the Cutty Sark is one of the few independent pubs left in Greenwich. Half a dozen cask-conditioned ales on tap line the bar, with an inviting riverside sitting-out area opposite. It's a 15-minute walk from the DLR station or hop on a bus along Trafalgar Rd and walk north. (www.cuttysarktavern.co.uk; 4-6 Ballast Quay, SE10; ☺11am-11pm Mon-Sat, noon-10.30 Sun; ℝDLR Cutty Sark)

Old Brewery   BAR

The Old Brewery (8 ✖ Map p166, B2) is run by the Meantime Brewery, selling its own draught Imperial Pale Ale (brewed on site), along with a heady range of more than 50 beers, from Belgian Trappist ales to fruity and smoked beers. We love the 'bottle chandelier' inside and the courtyard for sunny days. (www.oldbrewerygreenwich.com; Pepys Bldg, Old Royal Naval College, SE10; ☺11am-11pm Mon-Sat, noon-10.30pm Sun; ℝDLR Cutty Sark)

Greenwich Union   PUB

13 🍺 Map p166, B5

The award-winning Union plies six or seven local microbrewery beers, including raspberry and wheat varieties, and a strong list of ales, plus bottled international brews. It's a handsome place, with duffed-up leather armchairs and a welcoming long, narrow aspect that leads to the conservatory and beer garden at the rear. (www.greenwichunion.com; 56 Royal Hill; ☺noon-11pm Mon-Sat, 11.30am-10.30pm Sun; ℝDLR Cutty Sark)

Understand

Architectural Style

Greenwich is home to an extraordinary interrelated cluster of classical buildings. All the great architects of the Enlightenment made their mark here, largely due to royal patronage. In the early 17th century, Inigo Jones built one of England's first classical Renaissance homes, the Queen's House, which still stands. Charles II was particularly fond of the area and had Sir Christopher Wren build both the Royal Observatory and part of the Royal Naval College, which John Vanbrugh completed in the early 17th century.

Entertainment

Up the Creek   COMEDY

14 ⭐   Map p166, A3

Bizarrely enough, the hecklers can be funnier than the acts at this club. Mischief, rowdiness and excellent comedy are the norm with open mic nights on Thursdays (www.theopenmic.co.uk; £4), and Sunday specials (www.sundayspecial.co.uk; £6). There's an after-party disco on Fridays and Saturdays. (www.up-the-creek.com; 302 Creek Rd, SE10; admission £4-16; ⊙7.30-11pm Thu & Sun, to 2am Fri & Sat; ℝGreenwich, DLR Cutty Sark)

O2 Arena   LIVE MUSIC

15 ⭐   Map p166, D1

This major concert venue hosts all the biggies (the Rolling Stones, Britney Spears, Prince and many others) inside its 20,000-capacity stadium. It's also a popular venue for sporting events (tennis, horseriding etc). (www.theo2.co.uk; Peninsula Sq, SE10; ⊖North Greenwich)

Shopping

Greenwich Market   HANDICRAFTS

16 🔒   Map p166, B3

Greenwich may be one of the smallest of London's ubiquitous markets but it holds its own when it comes to quality: on Tuesdays, Wednesdays, Fridays and weekends, stallholders tend to be small, independent artists offering original prints, wholesome

Local Life

Greenwich Comedy Festival

Early September sees Greenwich split its sides playing host to London's largest comedy festival, the **Greenwich Comedy Festival** (www.greenwichcomedyfestival.co.uk), set in the grounds of the Old Royal Naval College.

beauty products, funky jewellery and accessories, cool fashion and so on. On Tuesdays, Thursdays and Fridays, it's vintage, antiques and collectables. (www.shopgreenwich.co.uk/greenwich-market; SE10; ⊙10am-5.30pm Tue-Sun)

Beehive   VINTAGE

17 🔒   Map p166, A3

Funky meeting ground of old vinyl (Bowie, Rolling Stones, vintage soul) and retro togs (frocks, leather jackets and overcoats). (320-322 Creek Rd, SE10; ⊙10.30am-6pm Tue-Sun; ℝDLR Cutty Sark)

Emporium   VINTAGE

18 🔒   Map p166, A3

Each piece is individual at this lovely vintage shop, where glass cabinets are crammed with costume jewellery, old perfume bottles and straw hats, while gorgeous jackets and blazers intermingle on the clothes racks. The men's offering is unusually good for vintage shops. (330-332 Creek Rd, SE10; ⊙10.30am-6pm Wed-Sun; ℝDLR Cutty Sark)

The Best of
London

Woman in costume, Notting Hill Carnival (p149)
JANE SWEENEY/GETTY IMAGES ©

Best Walks
Tower of London to the Tate Modern

🏃 The Walk

Commencing at one of London's most historic sights, this walk crosses the Thames at magnificent Tower Bridge, before heading west along the river, scooping up some excellent views and passing breathtaking modern architecture, history and Shakespeare's Globe. It comes to a halt amid the renowned art of the Tate Modern.

Start Tower of London; ⊖Tower Hill

Finish Tate Modern; ⊖Southwark, London Bridge

Length 3km; 90 minutes

🍴 Take a Break

On Fridays and Saturdays, grab take-away from one of the many stalls at Borough Market (p121). On other days, head to Applebee's Fish Cafe (p116) at the heart of the market, a fishmonger-cum-restaurant that will cook anything you fancy from its counter.

❶ Tower of London

Rising commandingly over the Thames, the ancient **Tower of London** (p84) enjoys a dramatic location. Be dazzled by the vast Koh-i-Noor diamond, explore the impressive White Tower and tag along with a Yeoman Warder on an enlightening tour.

❷ Tower Bridge

Cross ornate 19th-century **Tower Bridge** (p94) – traversed by more than 40,000 people daily – to the south side of the Thames. For information on the bridge (and brilliant views), enter the **Tower Bridge Exhibition**.

❸ HMS Belfast

Walk west along Queen's Walk past **City Hall** (p114), called the 'Leaning Tower of Pizzas' by some. Moored a bit further ahead, **HMS Belfast** (p113), a light cruiser that served in WWII and later conflicts, is a floating museum.

❹ Shard

Pop through the shopping complex of Hay's

RICHARD I'ANSON/GETTY IMAGES ©

Borough Market (p121)

Galleria to Tooley St to see the **Shard** (p114), designed by Italian architect Renzo Piano. Views from the tallest building in the European Union are breathtaking but come at a price.

5 Borough Market

Keep walking west along Tooley St, dip down Borough High St to head up Stoney St to **Borough Market** (p174), overflowing with tasty produce from Thursday to Saturday. If you fancy a beer, keep walking along Stoney

St to the **Rake** (p117) on Winchester Walk.

6 Southwark Cathedral

Southwark Cathedral (p114) is both fascinating and relaxing. Parts of the church date to medieval times and its treasured haul of artefacts includes a lovely Elizabethan sideboard and an icon of Jesus.

7 Shakespeare's Globe

Wander west along Clink St – and past the remains of Winchester

Palace – to Bankside and on to **Shakespeare's Globe** (p119). Join one of the tours if you have time.

8 Tate Modern

Not far west of Shakespeare's Globe is the **Millennium Bridge** (p112) and London's standout modern and contemporary art gallery, the **Tate Modern** (p106). The most dramatic entrance to the Tate Modern is off Holland St in the west, where you access the **Turbine Hall** down the ramp.

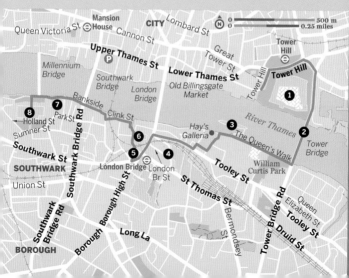

Best Walks
Royal London

🏃 The Walk

Lassoing in the cream of London's top royal and stately sights, this attraction-packed walk ticks off some of the city's truly must-do experiences on one comprehensive route. Don't forget to pack your camera – you'll be passing some of London's most famous buildings and historic sites, so photo opportunities abound. The walk conveniently returns you in a loop almost to your starting point for easy access to other parts of London.

Start Westminster Abbey; ⊖Westminster, St James's Park

Finish Banqueting House; ⊖Westminster

Length 3.5km; two hours

✕ Take a Break

Pack a picnic to eat in St James's Park (p34) if it's a sunny day. Alternatively, the same park's Inn the Park (p37) cafe and restaurant is a finely located choice for a meal, drink and excellent views.

Banqueting House (p35)

❶ Westminster Abbey

Start by exploring mighty **Westminster Abbey** (p24), preferably early (before the crowds). This is where almost every English sovereign since 1066 has been crowned.

❷ Churchill War Rooms

Walk around Parliament Sq, past the **UK Supreme Court** (it's free to sit in courtrooms during hearings) on the west side of the square, to the **Churchill War Rooms** (p34) to discover how Churchill coordinated the Allied war against Hitler.

❸ Buckingham Palace

Walking to the end of Birdcage Walk brings you to majestic **Buckingham Palace** (p28), where the state rooms are accessible to ticket-holders in August and September; alternatively pay a visit to the **Royal Mews** (p29) and the **Queen's Gallery** (p29), both nearby.

❹ St James's Park

Amble along The Mall and enter **St James's Park (**p176**)** – one of London's most attractive royal parks. Walk alongside **St James's Park Lake** for its plentiful ducks, geese, swans and other water fowl.

❺ Trafalgar Square

Return to The Mall and pass through **Admiralty Arch** to **Trafalgar Square** (p50) for regal views down Whitehall to the Houses of Parliament.

❻ Horse Guards Parade

Walk down Whitehall to the entrance to **Horse Guards Parade** (p35). The dashing mounted sentries of the Queen's Household Cavalry are on duty here daily from 10am to 4pm, when the dismounted guards are changed.

❼ Banqueting House

On the far side of the street, magnificent **Banqueting House** (p35) is the last surviving remnant of Whitehall

Palace, which once stretched most of the way down Whitehall but vanished in a late-17th-century fire. Further down Whitehall is the entrance to **No 10 Downing Street** (p36) and, beyond that, Parliament Sq and the **Houses of Parliament** (p30).

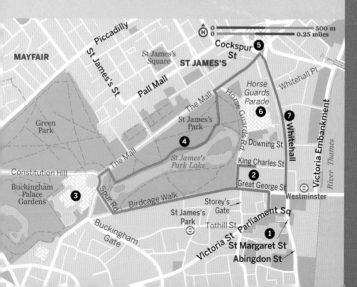

Best Walks
South Bank to the Houses of Parliament

🏃 The Walk

Packing some supreme views, this easily manage-able walk along the Thames kicks off at London's signature cultural hub – the Southbank Centre – before gravitating towards one of the city's most distinctive architectural gems: the Houses of Parliament. Along the way you will pass the iconic London Eye, elegant Westminster Bridge and some of the most superlative vistas the city can muster.

Start Southbank Centre; ⊖Waterloo, Embankment

Finish Jewel Tower; ⊖Westminster

Length 1.5km; one hour

✗ Take a Break

Pack a picnic to eat in Jubilee Gardens next to the London Eye or feast on the excellent cuisine at styl-ish Skylon (p115) at Royal Festival Hall.

London Eye (p113) and County Hall

RICHARD I'ANSON/GETTY IMAGES ©

❶ Southbank Centre

London's leading cultural landmark and the world's largest single-run arts centre, the **Southbank Centre** (p120) is anchored by the 1950s outline of the refurbished **Royal Festival Hall**. Bibliophiles may find themselves drawn to the **Southbank Centre Book Market** (p121) beneath the arches of Waterloo Bridge.

❷ London Eye

If you want to ride the **London Eye** (p113) – the huge Ferris wheel twirling above the Thames – you may need a fast-track ticket to get ahead of the queues. Alternatively, relax on the grass of **Jubilee Gardens** if the sun is shining or take in the buzzing street life: this is prime territory for street artists, from human statues to break-dancing acts.

❸ County Hall

Begun in 1909 but not completed until 1922, **County Hall** is an im-pressive building faced in Portland stone with first-rate views across the Thames to the Houses of Parliament. For many years, County Hall was the home of local government for London; today it houses the **Sea Life London Aquarium**, a film museum and hotels.

❹ Westminster Bridge

Completed in 1862, seven-arched **Westminster Bridge** is a later Gothic replacement for the 15-arch bridge of Portland stone upon which William Wordsworth penned his

sonnet *Composed upon Westminster Bridge, September 3, 1802*. Today's bridge features in the early scenes of horror film *28 Days Later*.

❺ Houses of Parliament

At the end of Westminster Bridge rises the elaborate Gothic stonework of the **Houses of Parliament** (p30), also called the Palace of Westminster. The three imposing towers of the Houses of Parliament are Elizabeth Tower (colloquially called '**Big Ben**'), Victoria Tower at

the southwestern corner and Central Tower between the two.

❻ Jewel Tower

With a history of over 700 years, the **Jewel Tower** stands on the far side of Abingdon St from Victoria Tower. The tower was one of two buildings (the other was Westminster Hall) that survived the 1834 fire that destroyed the Palace of Westminster. One of London's oldest surviving structures, the tower contains an exhibition on its history and functions.

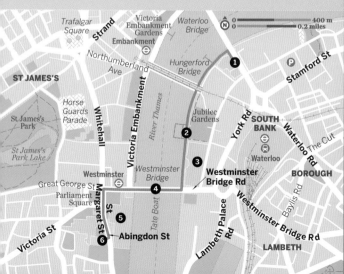

Best Eating

Once the laughing stock of the cooking world, London has got its culinary act together over the past two decades and is now an undisputed dining destination. There are plenty of fine, Michelin-starred restaurants, but it is the sheer variety on offer that is extraordinary: an A–Z of world cooking that is a culinary expression of the city's cultural diversity.

World Food

One of the joys of eating out in London is the profusion of choice. For historical reasons Indian cuisine is widely available (curry has been labelled a national dish), but Asian cuisines in general are very popular: Chinese, Thai, Japanese and Korean restaurants are all abundant, as well as elaborate fusion establishments blending flavours from different parts of Asia.

Food from continental Europe – French, Italian, Spanish, Greek, Scandinavian – is another favourite, with many classy Modern European establishments. Restaurants serving other types of cuisines tend to congregate where their home community is based.

Gastropubs

While not so long ago the pub was where you went for a drink, with maybe a packet of potato crisps to soak up the alcohol, the birth of the gastropub in the 1990s means that today just about every pub offers full meals. The quality varies widely, from defrosted on the premises to Michelin-star worthy.

SU-LIN LEE/GETTY IMAGES ©

☑ Top Tips

▶ Make reservations at weekends, particularly if you're in a group of more than four people.

▶ Top-end restaurants offer great value set lunch menus; à la carte prices are sometimes cheaper for lunch too.

▶ Many West End restaurants offer good-value pre- or post-theatre menus.

Best British

Launceston Place
Fantastic looks, outstanding food. (p143)

Dinner by Heston Blumenthal Celebration of British cuisine with both traditional and modern accents. (p143)

Skylon (p115)

Market Calming combination of bare brick walls and a classic, wholesome British menu. (p155)

St John The restaurant that inspired the revival of British cuisine. (p99)

Best European

Bocca di Lupo Sophisticated Italian cuisine in Soho. (p55)

Dabbous Head-spinning flavours in industrial chic decor. (p75)

Baltic Flavours from Eastern Europe on your plate as well as in your glass. (p115)

Best Asian

Yauatcha Top-drawer dim sum in a stylish, contemporary dining environment. (p53)

Dishoom Hugely successful revival of the old Bombay cafes. (p52)

Baozi Inn Beijing street food in vintage communist decor. (p55)

Abeno Delicious Japanese pancakes within a hop and skip of the British Museum. (p75)

Best for Views

Duck & Waffle Round-the-clock British fare with City views. (p96)

Skylon Stunning Thames vistas; fine international menu. (p178)

Worth a Trip

The fantastic **Providores & Tapa Room** (☎ 020-7935 6175; www.theprovidores.co.uk; 109 Marylebone High St, W1; 2/3/4/5 courses £33/47/57/63; ⏱ 9am-10.30pm Mon-Fri, 10am-10pm Sat & Sun; ⊖ Baker St) is split over two levels: tempting tapas (£2.50 to £17) on the ground floor (no bookings); and outstanding fusion cuisine in the elegant dining room above. There's a fantastic brunch on Saturdays and Sundays.

Best
Drinking &
Nightlife

There's little Londoners like to do more than party. From Hogarth's 18th-century Gin Lane prints to Mayor Boris Johnson's decision to ban all alcohol on public transport in 2008, the capital's obsession with drink and its effects shows absolutely no sign of waning. Some parts of London only come alive in the evening and surge through the early hours.

LATITUDESTOCK · CATH HARRIES/GETTY IMAGES ©

Pubs

At the heart of London social life, the pub (public house) is one of the capital's great social levellers. You can order almost anything you like, but beer is the staple. Some pubs specialise, offering drinks from local microbreweries, fruit beers, organic ciders and other rarer beverages; others proffer strong wine lists, especially gastropubs. Some pubs have delightful gardens – crucial in summer.

Most pubs and bars open at 11am and close at 11pm from Monday to Saturday and at 10.30pm on Sunday. Some pubs stay open longer, often midnight, sometimes 1am or 2am.

Bars & Clubs

Generally open later than pubs but closing earlier than clubs, bars tempt those keen to skip bedtime at 11pm but not up for clubbing. They may have DJs and a small dance floor, door charges after 11pm, more modern decor and fancier (and pricier) drinks, including cocktails, than pubs do. If you're for clubbing, London is an embarrassment of riches: choose between legendary establishments, such as Fabric, or smaller clubs with up-and-coming DJs.

☑ Top Tips

▶ Check the listings in *Time Out* (www.timeout.com/london), the *Evening Standard* (www.standard.co.uk) and *Resident Advisor* (www.residentadvisor.net).

▶ Dress to impress (no jeans or trainers) in posh clubs in areas like Kensington; further east, it's laid-back and edgy.

Best All-Round Pubs

Edinboro Castle Cultured Primrose Hill boozer with beer garden. (p156)

Lock Tavern Top Camden pub with roof terrace and live music. (p156)

Trafalgar Tavern (p169)

Greenwich Union Inviting Greenwich pub with strong beer menu. (p170)

Blackfriar Fine pub with distinctive, much-loved interior and bags of character. (p100)

Best Historic Pubs

George Inn History and age-old charm in spades. (p118)

Trafalgar Tavern With a distinguished pub pedigree, this is perfect for a riverside pint. (p169)

Cutty Sark Tavern Sip on a great range of ales down by the river. (p169)

Queen's Larder Classic Bloomsbury pub with royal connections and a cosy disposition. (p69)

Best Bars

London Cocktail Club Cocktails for the connoisseur. (p77)

Folly Secret bar-cum-garden in the heart of the city. (p99)

Galvin at Windows Twilight views through a raised cocktail. (p145)

French House Bohemian Soho bolt-hole with bundles of history. (p47)

Best Clubs

Fabric London's most famous superclub. (p100)

Heaven *The* gay club in London. (p57)

Kensington Roof Gardens Utterly divine: dress to impress and be prepared to queue. (p144)

Catch Guaranteed good night out in Shoreditch. (p103)

Best
Entertainment

Whatever soothes your soul, flicks your switch or floats your boat, from inspiring theatre to dazzling musicals, comedy venues, dance, opera or live music, London has an energetic and innovative answer. In fact, you could spend several lifetimes in London and still only sample a fraction of the astonishing range of entertainment on offer.

ROY RAINFORD/GETTY IMAGES ©

Theatre

A night at the theatre in London is a must-do experience. London's Theatreland in the West End has a concentration of English-speaking theatres (more than 40) rivalled only by New York's Broadway. With the longest history, London theatre is also the world's most diverse, from Shakespeare's classics to boundary-pushing productions, raise-the-roof musicals that run and run, or productions from tiny theatres stuffed away above pubs.

Classical Music

Music lovers will be spoiled for choice with London's four world-class symphony orchestras, two opera companies, smaller ensembles and fantastic venues (and reasonable ticket prices). The Southbank Centre, Barbican and Royal Albert Hall all maintain an alluring program of performances, with traditional crowd-pleasers as well as innovative compositions. The Proms (www.bbc.co.uk/proms) is the largest event on the festival calendar.

London Sounds

London has long generated edgy and creative sounds. There's live music – rock, blues, jazz, folk, whatever – going on every night of the week, from clubs to pubs or concert arenas.

☑ **Top Tips**

▶ Cut-price standby tickets are generally available at the National Theatre, the Barbican, the Southbank Centre and the Royal Opera House. Pick up in person on the day.

▶ Most mainstream and art-house cinemas offer discounts all day Monday and most weekday afternoon screenings.

Best Theatre

Shakespeare's Globe
For the authentic open-air Elizabethan effect. (p119)

National Theatre
Cutting-edge productions in three theatres. (p119)

Royal Albert Hall (p146)

Royal Court Theatre
Constantly innovative and inspirationally driven Sloane Sq theatre. (p146)

Best for Classical Music & Opera

Royal Albert Hall Splendid red-brick Victorian concert hall south of Kensington Gardens. (p146)

Southbank Centre London's leading performing arts venue, on the South Bank. (p120)

Royal Opera House The venue of choice for classical ballet and opera buffs. (p58)

Best for Live Jazz

Ronnie Scott's Legendary Frith St jazz club in the heart of the West End. (p58)

Pizza Express Jazz Club Big jazz names, pizazz and pizza. (p79)

Blues Kitchen Music for the ears, and smokin' New Orleans flavours on the plate. (p157)

Best Live Rock

12 Bar Rocking West End venue: small but packing a big punch. (p79)

Barfly Undersized but ambitious club with an ear for up-and-coming names. (p157)

Worth a Trip

Wigmore Hall (www.wigmore-hall.org.uk; 36 Wigmore St, W1; ⊖ Bond St) is one of the best concert venues in town for its fantastic acoustics, beautiful art nouveau hall, great variety of concerts and recitals and sheer standard of performances. Built in 1901 as the recital hall for Bechstein Pianos, it has remained one of the top places in the world for chamber music.

Best
Gay & Lesbian

SIMON GREENWOOD/GETTY IMAGES ©

The city of Oscar Wilde, Quentin Crisp and Elton John does not disappoint its gay visitors, proffering a fantastic mix of brash, camp, loud and edgy parties, bars, clubs and events year-round. It's a world capital of gaydom on par with New York and San Francisco: London's gay and lesbian communities have turned good times into an art form.

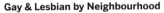

☑ Top Tip

▶ Check out www.gingerbeer.co.uk for the full low-down on lesbian events, club nights and bars.

Gay & Lesbian by Neighbourhood

Fashionable Shoreditch is home to London's more alternative gay scene, often very well mixed in with local straight people. The long-established gay village of Soho has lost some ground to the edgy East End.

Best Events

Lesbian & Gay Film Festival (www.bfi.org.uk/llgff) Hosted by the BFI Southbank in early April.

Pride (www.londoncommunitypride.org) In late June/early July, one of the world's largest gay pride events.

Best Bars & Clubs

Edge London's largest gay bar and seven-nights-a-week crowd pleaser. (p57)

Candy Bar One of Lesbian London's most enduringly popular bars. (p57)

Heaven Long-standing club and still a Saturday night magnet on the gay scene. (p57)

Best
Markets

The capital's famed markets are a treasure trove of small designers, unique jewellery, original framed photographs and posters, colourful vintage pieces, priceless vinyls and countless bric-a-brac gems. The antidote to impersonal, carbon-copy high-street shopping, most markets are outdoors, but they are always busy – rain or shine.

KIMBERLEY COOLE/GETTY IMAGES ©

☑ **Top Tip**

▶ Look out for plentiful freebie snack samples at Borough Market.

London Life

Shopping at London's markets isn't just about picking up bargains and rummaging through mounds of knick-knacks – although they give you plenty of opportunity to do that. It's also about taking in the character of this vibrant city: Londoners love to trawl through markets – browsing, chatting, socialising and grabbing lunch on the go.

Best Markets

Borough Market Bustling cornucopia of gastronomic delights, south of the river. (p174)

Maltby Street Market Low-key, fun, eccentric gathering of gourmet food stalls. (p115)

Portobello Market London's best-known market, in ever-hip Notting Hill. (p149)

Greenwich Market Fascinating for gift ideas or for highly moreish snacking on the go. (p171)

Camden Market North London's must-see market. (p159)

Best
Shops

From charity-shop finds to designer 'it bags', there are thousands of ways to spend your hard-earned cash in London. Many of the big-name shopping attractions, such as Harrods, Hamleys and Portobello Market have become must-sees in their own right, but chances are that with so many temptations, you'll give your wallet a full workout.

High Street Chains

Many shoppers bemoan chains taking over the high street, leaving independent shops struggling. But since the chains are cheap, fashionable and conveniently located, Londoners keep going back for more. As well as familiar overseas retailers, such as Gap, H&M, Urban Outfitters and Zara, you'll find a number of home-grown chains, including French Connection UK (www.frenchconnection.com), Jigsaw (www.jigsaw-online.com), Karen Millen (www.karenmillen.com), Marks & Spencer (www.marksandspencer.com), Miss Selfridge (www.missselfridge.com) and Topshop (www.topshop.com).

Opening Hours

London shops generally open from 9am or 10am to 6pm or 7pm Monday to Saturday. The majority of West End shops (Oxford St, Soho and Covent Garden), Chelsea, Knightsbridge, Kensington, Greenwich and Hampstead also open on Sunday, typically from noon to 6pm but sometimes 10am to 4pm. Shops in the West End open late (to 9pm) on Thursday; those in Chelsea, Knightsbridge and Kensington open late on Wednesday. If a major market is in swing on a certain day, neighbouring shops will probably also fling open their doors.

MATTHEW CHATTLE/ALAMY ©

☑ **Top Tip**

▶ In shops displaying a 'tax free' sign, visitors from non-EU countries are entitled to claim back the 20% value-added tax (VAT) they have paid on purchased goods.

Best Shopping Areas

West End Grand confluence of big names for the well heeled and well dressed. (p60)

Knightsbridge Harrods and other top names servicing London's incurable shopaholics. (p136)

Best Department Stores

Harrods Garish, stylish and just this side of

Harrods (p147)

kitsch, yet perennially popular. (p147)

Harvey Nichols Packed with sleek brand-name fashions, expensive fragrances, jewellery and more. (p137)

Liberty An irresistible blend of contemporary styles in an old-fashioned mock-Tudor atmosphere. (p60)

Fortnum & Mason London's oldest grocery store with staff still dressed in old-fashioned tailcoats. (p38)

Best for Books

John Sandoe Books A charmingly old-fashioned bookshop much loved by customers. (p137)

Stanford's Should be your first port of call for travel books. (p60)

Foyle's Sprawling bookshop with a vast range of reading (and listening) material. (p47)

Waterstone's Largest bookshop in Europe, with knowledgeable staff and regular author readings and signings. (p61)

Best for Gifts

Penhaligon's Beautiful range of perfumes and home fragrances, overseen by very helpful staff. (p38)

Shepherds Top quality stationery, fine paper, first-rate photograph albums and diaries. (p39)

Gallery One Highly original – and affordable – prints of London. (p61)

Worth a Trip

Dalston in northeast London has become something of a mecca for vintage shoppers. Recommended are high-end secondhand shop **Traid** (www.traid.org.uk; 106-108 Kingsland High St, E8; ⏲10am-6pm Mon-Sat, to 5pm Sun; 🚉Dalston Junction, Dalston Kingsland) and retro emporium **Beyond Retro** (www.beyondretro.com; 92-100 Stoke Newington Rd, N16; ⏲10am-7pm Mon-Wed, Fri & Sat, 10am-8pm Thu, 11.30am-6pm Sun; 🚉Dalston Kingsland, Dalston Junction).

Best
Museums & Galleries

WIBOWO RUSLI/GETTY IMAGES ©

London's museums and galleries top the list of the city's must-see attractions and not just for rainy days that frequently send locals scurrying for cover. Some of London's museums and galleries display incomparable collections that make them acknowledged leaders in their field.

Museums at Night

Nights are an excellent time to visit museums as there are fewer visitors. Many museums open late once or twice a week, and several organise special nocturnal events to extend their range of activities and present the collection in a different mood. Hop onto museum websites to see what's in store. (Some only arrange night events once a year, in May.)

Admission & Access

National museum collections (eg British Museum, National Gallery, Victoria & Albert Museum) are free, except for temporary exhibitions. Private galleries are usually free (or have a small admission fee), while smaller museums will charge an entrance fee, typically around £5 (book online at some museums for discounted tickets). National collections are generally open 10am to around 6pm, with one or two late nights a week.

Specialist Museums

Whether you've a penchant for fans, London transport or ancient surgical techniques, you'll discover museums throughout the city with their own niche collections. Even for non-specialists these museums can be fascinating to browse, and to share in the enthusiasm of the curators that's instilled in their collections.

☑ **Top Tip**

▶ Many of the top museums also have fantastic restaurants, worthy of a visit in their own right.

Best Collections (& All Free)

British Museum
Supreme collection of rare artefacts. (p64)

Victoria & Albert Museum Unique array of decorative arts and design in an awe-inspiring setting. (p128)

National Gallery
Tremendous gathering of largely pre-modern masters. (p44)

Tate Modern A feast of modern and contemporary art, wonderfully housed. (p106)

National Gallery (p44) at Trafalgar Square (p50)

Natural History Museum Major hit with kids and adults alike. (p132)

Best Small Museums

London Transport Museum An absorbing exploration of London's transport history. (p52)

Old Operating Theatre Museum & Herb Garrett Unique, eye-opening foray into old-fashioned surgery techniques. (p113)

Best Museum Architecture

Victoria & Albert Museum A building as beautiful as its diverse collection. (p128)

Natural History Museum Architectural lines straight from a Gothic fairy tale. (p132)

Tate Modern Disused power station transformed into iconic gallery. (p106)

Tate Britain Grandiose sibling of the Tate Modern. (p34)

National Maritime Museum Standout museum collection housed within wonderful architecture. (p167)

Worth a Trip

London's East End and Docklands area has gone through remarkable transformations in the past 150 years, from poor immigrant backwater to industrial powerhouse, through post-industrial depression to Olympic venue. Follow this tumultuous history at the **Museum of London Docklands** (www.museumoflondon.org.uk/docklands; Hertsmere Rd, West India Quay, E17; admission free; 10am-6pm; DLR West India Quay).

Best
Parks & Gardens

Glance at a colour map of London and be struck by how much is green – over a quarter of the city is made up of parks and gardens. Some of the world's most superb urban parkland is here: most of it well tended, accessible and delightful in any season.

Access & Activities

Usually free to access, London's royal and municipal parks are typically open from dawn till dusk. Larger parks, such as Regent's Park, may have football pitches and tennis courts. Or you might find options for playing golf, such as at Greenwich Park. Many have popular jogging routes or cycle tracks; larger, wilder expanses are ideal for cross-country running or orienteering.

If you have young kids, parks are ideal as most have playgrounds. Many parks are also venues for open-air concerts, sporting competitions and other fun outdoor events and activities, including horse riding (Hyde Park and Richmond Park), kite-flying and Frisbee-throwing.

An abundance of wildlife thrives in London parkland, especially in the larger parks with woodland and those with lakes (such as St James's Park), while the city's gardens (such as Kew Gardens) boast an astonishing range of plant life.

Heaths & Commons

Less formal or well-tended public spaces that can also be freely accessed are called commons or heaths. Wilder and more given over to nature than parks, the best-known heath is magnificent Hampstead Heath in North London.

Best Parks

Hyde Park Gorgeous, and massive, green paradise in the heart of Kensington. (p140)

St James's Park Enthralling views, splendid location and deckchairs to rent. (p176)

Greenwich Park Fine royal park graced with one of London's most superb viewpoints. (p167)

Regent's Park The most formal of London's royal parks, great for sports. (p154)

Best Gardens

Kew Gardens Astonishing range of botanical specimens and delightful views. (p41)

Kensington Gardens Highly desirable and good-looking appendage to Hyde Park. (p140)

Serpentine Cafe and Hyde Park (p140)

Wildlife Garden Pastoral pocket of greenery and wildlife in the heart of Kensington Palace. (p135)

Best Park & Garden Architecture

Kew Gardens Gorgeous Victorian glasshouse architecture, a palace, pagoda, Japanese gate and more. (p41)

Kensington Gardens One of London's best-loved palaces, a lavish Victorian memorial and famous art gallery. (p140)

Greenwich Park The Royal Observatory, Planetarium and delicious views over Greenwich's stately buildings. (p167)

Best Parks for Activities

Regent's Park Football, tennis, rugby, cricket and boating. (p154)

Hampstead Heath Swimming, running, kite-flying. (p160)

Worth a Trip

Covering almost 10 sq km, **Richmond Park** (⏱7am-dusk Mar-Sep, 7.30am-dusk Oct-Feb; ⊖Richmond) is the largest urban parkland in Europe, offering everything from formal gardens and ancient oaks to unsurpassed views of central London 12 miles away. Herds of more than 600 red and fallow deer basking under the trees add their own magic.

Best
Architecture

London is dotted with architectural gems from every period of its long history. This is a city for explorers: keep your eyes peeled and you'll spot part of a Roman wall enclosed in the lobby of a postmodern building near St Paul's, say, or a galleried coaching inn dating from the Restoration tucked away in a courtyard off a high street in Borough.

London Style

Unlike other world-class cities, London was never methodically planned, despite being largely burned to the ground in 1666. The city has instead developed in an organic (read: haphazard) fashion. This means that, although you can easily lose track of its historical narrative, a multitude of stories is going on all around you, creating a handsome patchwork that ranges across centuries.

London's New Skyscrapers

The Olympic effect saw a sudden scramble for high-altitude towers that would shake up the otherwise low-lying London skyline. Most famous is the Shard, rising over London Bridge like a vast glass splinter. The City of London's tallest building, the straight-edged Heron Tower, was completed just up the road from the Gherkin (30 St Mary Axe) in 2011. Aiming for a 2014 completion date, the top-heavy Walkie Talkie, aka 20 Fenchurch St, will be topped with a vast sky garden boasting magnificent views. Further construction on the concrete stub of the radical looking Pinnacle (22–24 Bishopsgate) – nicknamed the Helter Skelter due to its cork-screwing top – was on hold at the the time of writing.

DAVID C TOMLINSON/GETTY IMAGES ©

☑ Top Tip

▶ For one weekend every year, hundreds of buildings normally closed to the public throw their doors open for **Open House London** (☎020-3006 7008; www.londonopenhouse. org). Public buildings aren't forgotten either, with plenty of talks and tours.

Best Modern Architecture

30 St Mary Axe The bullet-shaped Gherkin, iconic tower of the City. (p94)

Shard Rising triumphantly over London Bridge since 2012. (p114)

Tate Modern Former power station; now

Hampton Court Palace (p122)

powerhouse of modern art. (p106)

Millennium Bridge
Elegant and sleek span across the Thames. (p112)

City Hall 'Glass gonad' or 'Darth Vader's Helmet'? Your call. (p114)

Best Early Architecture

Westminster Abbey
Titanic milestone in London's ecclesiastical architectural history. (p24)

Houses of Parliament
Westminster Hall is one of the finest hammer-beam roofs in the world. (p30)

Tower of London
Legend, myth and blood-stained history converge

in London's supreme bastion. (p84)

All Hallows by the Tower Fragments from Roman times in one of London's oldest churches. (p94)

Best Stately Architecture

Buckingham Palace
The Queen's pied-à-terre. (p28)

Houses of Parliament
Extraordinary Victorian monument and seat of British parliamentary democracy. (p30)

Queen's House Beautiful Inigo Jones Palladian creation in charming Greenwich. (p167)

Old Royal Naval College Admire the stunning Painted Hall

and breathtaking Chapel. (p168)

Hampton Court Palace
Get lost in the famous maze or ghost-hunt along Tudor hallways. (p123)

Best Monuments

Monument Spiral your way to the top for panoramic views. (p94)

Albert Memorial Convoluted and admirably excessive chunk of Victoriana. (p141)

Wellington Arch Topped by Europe's largest bronze sculpture. (p141)

Nelson's Column Kids will give their eye teeth to climb on the four lions. (p50)

Best
For Kids

London is a fantastic place for children. The city's museums will fascinate all ages, and you'll find theatre, dance and music performances perfect for older kids and teens. Playgrounds and outdoor spaces, such as parks, city farms and nature reserves are perfect for either toddler energy-busting or relaxation.

Museum Activities

London's museums are nothing if not child friendly. You'll find storytelling at the National Gallery, arts and crafts workshops at the Victoria & Albert Museum, train-making workshops at the London Transport Museum plus tons of finger-painting opportunities at Tate Modern and Tate Britain. Also check museum websites for details on popular sleepovers at the British Museum, the Natural History Museum, the Science Museum and other museums.

Eating with Kids

Many of London's restaurants and cafes are child-friendly and offer baby-changing facilities and high chairs. Pick your places with some awareness – avoid high-end and quieter, smaller restaurants and cafes if you have toddlers or babies, and go for noisier/more relaxed places and you'll find that you'll be welcomed.

London is a great opportunity for your kids to taste all the world's cuisines in close proximity, so pick from good-quality (and MSG-free) Chinese, to Italian, French, Mexican, Japanese and Indian restaurants. Many places have kids' menus, but ask for smaller portions of adult dishes if your children have a more adventurous palate; you'll find that most places will be keen to oblige.

MIKE BIRKHEAD/GETTY IMAGES ©

☑ Top Tips

▶ Under-11s travel free on the tube and bus and under-5s go free on the trains.

▶ In winter months (November to January), ice rinks appear at the Natural History Museum, Kew Gardens, Somerset House, the Tower of London and Hampton Court Palace.

Best Sights for Kids

Cutty Sark Explore a real ship and learn about its history sailing the high seas. (p167)

London Zoo Close to 750 species of animals, and an excellent Penguin Beach. (p154)

Science Museum (p140)

London Eye Survey London from altitude and tick off the big sights. (p113)

London Dungeon Squeamish fun, London's famous villains and chilling thrills. (p112)

Best Museums for Kids

Science Museum
Bursting with imaginative distractions for technical tykes, plus a fun-filled basement for little ones. (p140)

Imperial War Museum
Packed with exciting displays, war planes and military whatnot. (p112)

British Museum
Meet the mummies at London's best museum. (p64)

Natural History Museum Gawp at the animatronic *T. rex* and the thrilling Dinosaur Gallery. (p132)

Best Restaurants for Kids

Inn the Park Accommodating staff and plenty of space to run around between courses. (p176)

Old Brewery Popular with local families; toys and facilities galore. (p169)

Chin Chin Labs Scrumptious spectacular ice cream. (p155)

North Sea Fish Restaurant Can't go wrong with perfectly executed fish and chips. (p76)

Worth a Trip
Older kids and teenagers will love posing with life-like wax models of celebrities at **Madame Tussauds** (☎0870 400 3000; www.madame-tussauds. co.uk; Marylebone Rd, NW1; adult/child £30/26; ⊙9/10am-5/7pm (seasonal); ⊖Baker St). Be they members of the Royal Family, singers, actors, footballers or politicians, they're all there.

Best
Views

With its historical domes, skyscrapers and green hills, it's not hard to find bird's eye views of London – and what a sight the city's skyline makes. Some views come free, others at a price, others with a meal. Just make sure you pick a bright day to make the best of it.

GETTY IMAGES ©

Best Hill Views

Greenwich Park Clamber up to the Royal Observatory for sweeping views. (p167)

Parliament Hill Choice panoramas over London from the north of town. (p160)

Best Views from Structures

London Eye The perfect perspective on town. (p113)

Monument Wraparound, 360° views await your ascent to the top. (p94)

St Paul's Cathedral Clamber up into the dome for some of London's finest views. (p88)

Rhizotron & Xstrata Treetop Walkway Staggering views over the Victorian glasshouses and into Kew Gardens. (p41)

Shard Lego-like views of the city from the South Bank of the Thames. (p114)

Westminster Cathedral Impressive views over London from the tower of this fascinating cathedral. (p142)

Best Restaurant Views

Oxo Tower Restaurant & Brasserie Grab a front row seat for top views across the Thames. (p117)

Skylon Tuck into some of the best river views from a restaurant in town. (p117)

Portrait Like the restaurant, the views are a picture. (p53)

Duck & Waffle Great City views, open 24 hours a day. (p96)

Best Bar Views

Vertigo 42 Hope for clear skies and settle down for the bravura performance of sunset. (p100)

Galvin at Windows The Hyde Park perspective and high altitude combine to work wonders. (p145)

Cutty Sark Tavern Historic Greenwich pub with an eye-catching riverside position. (p169)

Best
Tours

Best Boat Tours

Thames River Boats
(☎020-7930 2062; www.
wpsa.co.uk; Westminster
Pier, Victoria Embankment,
SW1; Kew adult/child/family
one way £12/6/30, return
£18/9/45, Hampton Court
one way £15/7.50/37.50,
return £22.50/11.25/56.25;
⏰11am & 2pm Apr-Oct)
Boats from Westminster Pier to the Royal
Botanic Gardens at Kew
(1½ hours) and on to
Hampton Court Palace
(another 1½ hours, noon
boat only).

Thames River Services
(www.thamesriverservices.
co.uk; adult/child single
£12/6, return £15.50/7.75)
Cruise boats leaving
Westminster Pier for
Greenwich, stopping at
the Tower of London.

Best Bus Tours

Big Bus Tours (www.
bigbustours.com; adult/
child/family £29/12/70;
⏰every 20min 8.30am-
6pm Apr-Sep, to 5pm Oct
& Mar, to 4.30pm Nov-Feb)
Informative commentaries in eight languages;

ticket includes a free
river cruise and three
thematic walking tours.

Original Tour (www.theoriginaltour.com; adult/child/
family £26/13/91; ⏰every
20min 8.30am-5.30pm)
Open-top hop-on, hop-off bus tour, complete
with river cruise and
thematic walking tours.

Best Walking Tours

Association of Professional Tourist Guides
(APTG; ☎020-7611 2545;
www.touristguides.org.uk;
half-/full-day £127/200;
🚇Holborn) Hire a prestigious Blue Badge Guide
(know-it-all guides).

London Walks (☎020-
7624 3978; www.walks.com;
adult £9) A huge array
of walks, including Jack
the Ripper tours, Beatles
tours, a Harry Potter
locations tour and a
Sherlock Holmes tour.

London Mystery Walks
(☎07957 388280; www.
tourguides.org.uk; adult/
child £10/9) Tour Jack the
Ripper's old haunts. You
must book in advance.

CULTURA ASIA/GARY JOHN NORMAN/GETTY IMAGES ©

Open City (☎020-7383
2131; www.open-city.org.
uk; tours £14.50-35.50)
This charity organises
architectural tours to one
of four different areas
(Square Mile, South
London, the West End or
Docklands) weekly.

Best
Hidden Sights

London sightseeing might seem to be all about ticking off the big ticket sights, but the city is also full of attractions tucked away from the crowds. Tracking them down is an opportunity to get off the beaten trail, a chance to unearth the bizarre, concealed or simply unexpected.

SECRET CINEMA ©

Secret London

You might be surprised to find some of London's hidden sights just steps away from a drawcard sight, while others are entirely worthy of an expedition in themselves. From specialist museums to an early 19th-century windmill in Brixton, a Chinese pagoda, canal-side walks and Gothic tombstones, London's unexpected treasures range across genres.

Admission

Some of London's unexpected treats are entirely free to explore, while others – especially the tours – carry a fee and may need to be booked in advance, or as part of a group.

☑ Top Tips

▶ **Secret Cinema** (www.secretcinema. org) arranges films and locations that are secret till disclosed on the day of screening (which could be in a cemetery, a park, a warehouse, wherever), creating a sense of mystery and adventure.

Best Unusual Sights

Fan Museum An absorbing specialist collection of the 3000-year old device. (p168)

St Pancras Chambers Take a tour of this exquisite Victorian hotel, backdrop to numerous films and music videos. (p73)

Old Operating Theatre Museum & Herb Garret Get to grips with surgical techniques of yesteryear. (p113)

Wellcome Collection Captivating and intriguingly eclectic collection of miscellanea. (p72)

Greenwich Foot Tunnel Walk under the Thames from Greenwich to the Isle of Dogs. (p167)

Best Hidden London Gems

Michelin House Beautiful art nouveau treasure buried along Fulham Rd. (p142)

Chinese Pagoda Stunning 250-year old Oriental addition to the famous gardens at Kew. (p41)

Highgate Cemetery (p161)

Westminster Cathedral
An often overlooked interior dappled with moments of dazzling beauty. (p142)

Bedford Square Soak up the charms of London's best-preserved Georgian square. (p78)

Electric Cinema London's oldest cinema is as classic as much of its repertoire. (p149)

Best Behind-the-Scenes Tours

Tower of London Lets the world into the vault of the Crown Jewels at the Ceremony of the Keys at 9am. (p84)

Highgate Cemetery
Explore the sublimely overgrown western part of the cemetery. (p161)

St Paul's Cathedral
Snatch a look at the marvellous Geometric Staircase and the Quire. (p88)

Albert Memorial Hop over the barrier for closer scrutiny of the Frieze of Parnassus. (p141)

Best Hidden London Walks

Walking along Regent's Canal Sample London's canal-side charms from Camden to Little Venice. (p154)

Literary Bloomsbury
Follow in the footsteps of the literati around good-looking Bloomsbury. (p68)

Worth a Trip

Built for one John Ashby in 1816, **Brixton Windmill** (www.brixtonwindmill.org; Blenheim Gardens, SW2; ⊖ Brixton, then bus 45 or 59) is the closest windmill to central London still in existence. It was powered by gas in its later years and milled as recently as 1934. It's been refitted with sails and machinery for a wind-driven mill and is occasionally open for tours (check website for details), or you can simply admire it from the outside.

Best
Churches

London's churches vault the centuries from ancient times to the modern day in a greater concentration than anywhere else in the UK. Ranging across the denominations, London's houses of worship constitute some of the best examples of rare historic architecture in town, from the Saxon remnants of All Hallows by the Tower to the mighty stonework of St Paul's Cathedral and Westminster Abbey.

GETTY IMAGES ©

☑ Top Tip

▶ Churches can be excellent venues for free music recitals.

Loss & Survival

Hundreds of London churches have vanished over the centuries – especially during the Great Fire of London and the Blitz of WWII – but great numbers of them also managed to survive. Some churches, such as St Paul's Cathedral, were badly damaged but then rebuilt in an entirely different and more modern style. Others – such as St James's Piccadilly – were badly damaged during WWII and then gradually restored. A large number of London's churches, such as Southwark Cathedral, embrace architectural fragments of vastly different eras that trace the history of London in their stonework, from the middle ages to the modern day.

Best Large Churches

St Paul's Cathedral
London's most famous and enduring ecclesiastical icon. (p88)

Westminster Abbey
Hallowed site of coronation for England's sovereigns since William the Conqueror. (p24)

Southwark Cathedral
Spanning the centuries from the Normans to the Victorian era and beyond. (p114)

Westminster Cathedral Byzantine mosaics glitter within its sombre, unfinished interior. (p142)

Best Historic Churches

All Hallows by the Tower City church with a Saxon crypt and intriguing fragments from the Roman era. (p94)

St Bartholomew-the-Great Authentic Norman remains and an age-old sense of tranquillity. (p97)

St Stephen Walbrook A 17th-century Wren masterpiece in the City. (p96)

St Mary-le-Bow Another elegant ecclesiastical triumph from Sir Christopher Wren. (p97)

Southwark Cathedral (p114)

Best Churches for Free Recitals

St Martin-in-the-Fields
Hosts free concerts at 1pm on Monday, Tuesday and Friday. (p52)

St George's, Bloomsbury Check website for details of the church's program of concerts, some of which are free. (p74)

Best Church Cafes & Restaurants

Restaurant at St Paul's Modern British fare in a classic setting. (p89)

Café Below Cafe with oodles of atmosphere in the crypt of St Mary-le-Bow. (p97)

Crypt Café Excellent cafe with tombstone flooring in St Paul's. (p89)

Worth a Trip

Magnificent **Temple Church** (☎ 020-7353 8559; www.templechurch.com; Temple, EC4; adult/concession £4/2; ☺ 11am-1pm & 2-4pm Mon-Fri, hrs vary) was built by the Knights Templar. The church has a distinctive design: the Round (consecrated in 1185 and designed to recall the Church of the Holy Sepulchre in Jerusalem) adjoins the Chancel, the heart of the church. Both were severely damaged by a bomb in 1941 and reconstructed.

Best
Festivals &
Events

London is a vibrant city all year round, celebrating both traditional and modern festivals and events with energy and gusto. From Europe's largest outdoor carnival to the blooms of the Chelsea Flower Show and the pomp and ceremony of Trooping the Colour, London has entertaining occasions for all tastes.

FRANK FELL/GETTY IMAGES ©

Best Free Festivals

Notting Hill Carnival
London's most vibrant outdoor carnival is a celebration of Caribbean London; in August. (p149)

Chinese New Year
Chinatown fizzes in this colourful street festival; in late January or February.

Trooping the Colour
The Queen's official birthday in June sees parades and pageantry; at Horse Guards Parade.

Guy Fawkes' Night (Bonfire Night) Commemorates Guy Fawkes' attempt to blow up parliament in 1605, with bonfires and fireworks on 5 November.

Lord Mayor's Show
(www.lordmayorsshow. org) Floats, bands and fireworks to celebrate the Lord Mayor of the City; in November.

New Year On 31 December the famous countdown to midnight in Trafalgar Sq is met with terrific fireworks.

Best Ticketed Events

Wimbledon Lawn Tennis Championships
(www.wimbledon.com) Centre of the tennis universe for two weeks in June/July.

The Proms (www.bbc. co.uk/proms) Classical concerts around the Royal Albert Hall; in July to September.

London Film Festival
(www.bfi.org.uk/lff) Premier film event held at the BFI Southbank and other venues; in October.

☑ **Top Tip**

▶ For a list of events in and around London, check www. visitlondon.com or www.timeout.com/ london.

Chelsea Flower Show
(www.rhs.org.uk/chelsea) Renowned horticultural show, attracting the cream of West London society; in May.

Survival Guide

Survival Guide

Before You Go

When to Go

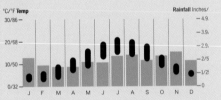

°C/°F Temp
30/86 —
20/68 —
10/50 —
0/32 —

Rainfall Inches/
— 4.9.
— 3.9.
— 2.9.
— 2/5
— 1/2!
— 0

J F M A M J J A S O N D

➡ **Winter (Dec-Feb)**
Cold, short days with much rain and occasional snow. Museums and attractions quieter and prices lower.

➡ **Spring (Mar-May)**
Mild, wet; trees in blossom. Major sights begin to get busy; parks starting to look lovely.

➡ **Summer (Jun-Aug)**
Warm to hot, sunny with long days. Main tourist and holiday season. Sights can be crowded but parks are lovely.

➡ **Autumn (Sep-Nov)**
Mild, generally sunny, good-looking season. Kids back at school, London quietens down after summer.

Book Your Stay

➡ Great neighbourhoods to stay in are around the National Gallery & Covent Garden, Kensington, St Paul's & the City and the South Bank.

➡ Bed and breakfasts come in a tier below hotels, but can have boutique-style charm, a lovely old building setting and a personal level of service.

➡ There are some fantastic hotels in London, but demand can often outstrip supply – especially at the bottom end of the market – so book ahead, particularly during holiday periods and in summer.

➡ Under £100 per night you'll be limited to mostly B&Bs and hostels. Look out, though, for weekend deals in City hotels that can put a better class of hotel within reach.

➡ If you're in London for a week or more, a short-term or serviced apartment can be economical and gives you more sense of living in the city.

Useful Websites

Lonely Planet (www.lonelyplanet.com/england/london/hotels) Bookings.

YHA Central Reservations System (📞0800 019 1700; www.yha.org.uk) Hostel room bookings.

Visit London (📞0871 222 3118; www.visitlondonoffers.com) London tourist organisation offering special deals and a list of gay-friendly accommodation.

LondonTown (📞020-7437 4370; www.londontown.com) Hotel bookings and deals.

Best Budget

Clink78 (📞020-7183 9400; www.clinkhostels.com; 78 King's Cross Rd, WC1; dm/r from £9/40; @🛜; ⊖King's Cross/St Pancras) Historic building and top-notch facilities in the up-and-coming King's Cross area.

Church Street Hotel (📞020-7703 5984; www.churchstreethotel.com; 29-33 Camberwell Church St, SE5; £60-90, d £90-170, f £190; ✳🛜🅿; 🚈Denmark Hill) A hot of Mexican panache

in South London matched by fantastic service.

Tune Hotel (www.tunehotels.com; r from £55) Spruce, clean, neat and pared down; pay for extras as required. Four branches in town.

YHA Oxford St (📞020-7734 1618; www.yha.org.uk; 14 Noel St, W1; dm/tw from £18/46; @🛜; ⊖Oxford Circus) Super central location and great facilities to boot, a bargain.

Best Midrange

Hoxton Hotel (📞020-7550 1000; www.hoxtonhotels.com; 81 Great Eastern St, EC2; d & tw £59-199; @🛜; ⊖Old St) Get top bang for your buck at this trendy hotel in the hip neighbourhood of Shoreditch.

Citizen M (📞020-3519 1680; www.citizenm.com/london-bankside; 20 Lavington St, SE1; r £109-189; ✳@🛜; ⊖Southwark) Sleek design, whizz-bang technology and lovely creature comforts, Citizen M ticks all the boxes.

La Suite West (📞020-7313 8484; www.lasuitewest.com; 41-51 Inverness Tce; r £130-354; ✳@🛜; ⊖Bayswater) Minimalist heaven in West London,

with impeccable interiors and garden suites.

Dean Street Townhouse (📞020-7434 1775; www.deanstreettownhouse.com; 69-71 Dean St, W1; r £180-440; ✳🛜; ⊖Tottenham Court Rd) Wonderful boudoir atmosphere with Georgian furniture and retro bathrooms in the heart of Soho.

Best Top-End

Dorset Square Hotel (📞020-7723 7874; www.firmdalehotels.com; 39 Dorset Sq, NW1; d from £260, ste from £350; ✳🛜; ⊖Baker St) Dreamy decor blending antiques, sumptuous fabrics and crown-canopied or four-poster beds.

Goring (📞020-7396 9000; www.thegoring.com; Beeston Place; r £540-1090; ⊖Victoria) If it's good enough for Kate Middleton, it's good enough for us! Think classy English style.

Rookery (📞020-7336 0931; www.rookeryhotel.com; 12 Peter's Lane, Cowcross St, EC1; s £235, d £238-625; ✳🛜; ⊖Farringdon) A splendid row of 18th-century Georgian houses, fitted out with antique furniture and handpicked artworks.

Great Northern Hotel
(020-3388 0800; www.
gnhlondon.com; King's Cross
Rd, N1; r from £300; ❄ 🛜;
 King's Cross/St Pancras)
The world's first railway
hotel, refurbished with
a boutique, classic style
reminiscent of luxury
sleeper trains.

Arriving in London

☑ **Top Tip** For the best
way to get to your neigh-
bourhood, see p17.

Heathrow Airport

Some 15 miles west
of central London,
Heathrow (LHR; www.
heathrowairport.com) is the
world's busiest interna-
tional airport, with five
terminals. Each terminal
has currency-exchange
facilities, information
counters and accommo-
dation desks.

➡ **Underground** (www.
tfl.gov.uk) The Piccadilly
line (£5, one hour from
central London) runs
from just after 5/5.45am
from/to the airport
(5.50/7am Sunday)

to 11.45pm/12.30am
(11.30pm Sunday in both
directions).

➡ **Heathrow Express**
(www.heathrowexpress.
com; one way/return
£20/34, 15 minutes, every 15
minutes) This train runs
from Heathrow Central
station to Paddington
station. Trains run from
approximately just after
5am in both directions,
and until 11.45pm (from
Paddington) and just
after midnight (from the
airport).

➡ **Heathrow Connect**
(www.heathrowconnect.com;
one way £9.50, 25 minutes,
every half hour) Travelling
between Heathrow and
Paddington station, this
train service makes five
stops en route. First
trains leave Heathrow at
about 5.20am (6am Sun-
day); last service is just
after 11pm. From Pad-
dington, services leave
between approximately
5am (6am Sunday) and
11pm.

➡ **Taxi** A metered black-
cab trip to/from central
London costs between
£45 and £65 (£60 from
Oxford St), and takes 45
to 60 minutes.

➡ **National Express**
(www.nationalexpress.com)
Coaches (one way/return

from £5/9; 45 minutes
to 90 minutes; frequency
is every 30 minutes to
one hour) regularly link
the Heathrow Central
Bus Station with **Victoria
coach station** (Map p138
G5; 164 Buckingham Palace
Rd, SW1; Victoria). The
first bus from Heathrow
Central Bus station (at
Terminals 1, 2 and 3) is
at 5.25am, the last at
9.40pm. The first bus
leaves Victoria at 7.45am,
the last at 11.30pm.

➡ **Night bus** N9 bus
(£1.40, 1¼ hr, every
20 minutes) connects
Heathrow with central
London.

Gatwick Airport

Some 30 miles south of
central London, Gatwick
is smaller than Heathrow.
The North and South Ter-
minals are linked by a 24-
hour shuttle train (about
a three-minute journey
between terminals).

➡ **National Rail** (0845
748 4950; www.nationalrail.
co.uk) Regular train
services to/from London
Bridge (30 minutes,
every 15 to 30 minutes),
King's Cross (55 minutes
every 15 to 30 minutes)
and London Victoria (30
minutes, every 10 to 15

minutes). Fares vary, allow £8 to £10 for a single.

➡ **Gatwick Express** (www.gatwickexpress.com; one way/return £19.90/34.90, 30 minutes, every 15 minutes) Train service from station near South Terminal to Victoria station. From Gatwick, services run between about 4.30am and 1.35am. From Victoria, they leave between 3.30am and 12.30am.

➡ **National Express** (www.nationalexpress.com) Coaches (one way from £7, 65 to 90 minutes) run between Gatwick to Victoria coach station at least once an hour between 6am and 9.45pm (fewer services till 11.30pm).

➡ **easyBus** (www.easybus.co.uk; one way £10, return from £12) Budget 19-seater minibuses (75 minutes, every 10 to 20 minutes) from Earl's Court/West Brompton to Gatwick, 3am to 12.30am daily. Departures from Gatwick between 4.20am and 1.30am. Tickets can be purchased from the driver (also at ticket outlets at the airport in both the North and South Terminals).

➡ **Taxi** A metered trip to/from central London

costs about £100 (and takes just over an hour).

St Pancras International Station

Eurostar (www.eurostar.com) The high-speed passenger rail service links St Pancras International station with Gare du Nord in Paris (two hours) or Bruxelles Midi in Brussels (less than two hours). King's Cross St Pancras is on the Victoria, Piccadilly, Northern, Hammersmith & City, Circle and Metropolitan Lines on the Underground.

Getting Around

Public transport in London is excellent, if pricey. Managed by **Transport for London** (www.tfl.gov.uk), it has a great, multilingual website with live updates on traffic, a journey planner, maps and information on all modes of transport. The cheapest way to travel across the network is with an Oyster Card.

Underground, DLR & Overground

☑ **Best for...**getting around quickly and easily.

➡ There are several networks: London Underground ('the tube'; 11 colour-coded lines), Docklands Light Railway (DLR, a driverless train operating in the eastern part of the city) and Overground trains.

➡ First trains operate around 5.30am Monday to Saturday and 7am Sunday. The last trains leave around 12.30am Monday to Saturday and 11.30pm Sunday.

➡ London is divided into nine concentric fare zones.

➡ It's always cheaper to travel with an Oyster card than a paper ticket.

➡ Children under the age of 11 travel free.

Bus

☑ **Best for...**London views and for going where the Underground doesn't run.

➡ Bus services normally operate from 5am to 11.30pm.

➡ Oyster cards are valid on all bus services, including night buses, and

Travel Passes & Tickets

Oyster cards are chargeable smart cards valid across the entire London public transport network. Fares for Oyster-card users are lower than standard tickets. If you are making many journeys during the day, you never pay more than the appropriate Travelcard fare (peak or off peak) once the daily 'price cap' is reached. Paper single and return tickets still exist but are substantially more expensive than using Oyster. Oyster cards for visitors are pre-loaded with credit and ready to use.

➡ Touch your card on a reader upon entry and then touch again on your way out. Credit is deducted accordingly. For bus journeys, just touch once upon boarding.

➡ Oyster cards are purchasable (£5 refundable deposit) and topped up at any Underground station, travel info centre or shop displaying the Oyster logo.

➡ Simply return your Oyster card at a ticket booth to get your deposit back, as well as any remaining credit.

➡ Day Travelcards are no cheaper than Oyster cards on the Underground, DLR, Overground and buses.

are cheaper than cash fares. If you only travel by bus, the daily cap is £4.40. Bus journeys cost a flat fare (non-Oyster/Oyster £2.40/1.40) regardless of how far you go.

➡ At bus stops with a yellow background, if you don't have an Oyster card, you must buy your ticket *before* boarding

the bus at the stop's ticket machine (you will need the exact amount in coins).

➡ Children under 11 travel free.

➡ Excellent 'bus spider maps' at every stop detail all routes and destinations available from that particular area.

➡ For interactive online bus maps, click on www.tfl.gov.uk.

➡ More than 50 night bus routes (prefixed with the letter 'N') run from 11pm to 5am.

➡ Another 60 bus routes run 24-hours; the frequency decreases between 11pm and 5am.

Bicycle

☑ **Best for...**short distances, although traffic can be intimidating.

➡ **Barclays Cycle Hire** (☎0845 026 3630; www.tfl.gov.uk.) is straightforward and particularly useful for visitors.

➡ Pick up a bike from one of the 570 docking stations dotted around the capital. Drop it off at another docking station.

➡ The access fee is £2/10 for 24 hours/a week. Insert your debit or credit card in the docking station to pay your access fee.

➡ The first 30 minutes is free, then it's £1 for the first hour, £4 up to two hours etc (the pricing structure encourages short journeys).

➡ Take as many bikes as you like during your

access period (24 hours/ one week), leaving five minutes between each trip.

➡ If the docking station is full, consult the terminal to find available docking points nearby.

➡ You must be 18 to buy access and at least 14 to ride a bike.

Taxi
☑ **Best for...**late nights and groups to share the cost.

➡ Fully licensed **London Black Cabs** (www. londonblackcabs.co.uk) are available for hire when the yellow sign above the windscreen is lit; just stick your arm out to signal one.

➡ Fares are metered, with a flag-fall charge of £2.40, rising by increments of 20p for each subsequent 168m.

➡ Fares are more expensive in the evenings and overnight.

➡ You can tip taxi drivers up to 10% but few Londoners do, simply rounding up to the nearest pound instead.

➡ **Hailo** (hailocab.com) uses GPS to connect your mobile phone to that of

the nearest free black-cab driver; download the free app from its website. You pay only the metered fare.

➡ Minicabs cannot be flagged but must be hired by phone or directly from one of the minicab offices (every high street has one and most hotels and clubs work with a minicab firm).

➡ Minicabs are usually cheaper than black cabs and don't have meters; the fare is set by the dispatcher.

Boat
☑ **Best for...**views.

➡ **Thames Clippers** (www. thamesclippers.com) boats are fast and you're always guaranteed a seat and a view.

➡ Boats run from 6am to just after 10pm, every 20 to 30 minutes, from London Eye Millennium Pier to Woolwich Arsenal Pier and points in between. Fares cost £6.50/3.25 for adults/children; there are discounts for Oyster card holders and travel card holders.

➡ There are sightseeing boat tours on the Thames, including boats

to Hampton Court Palace and Kew Gardens.

Car & Motorcycle
☑ **Best for...**getting out of London.

➡ Expensive parking charges, traffic jams, high petrol prices, efficient traffic wardens and wheel clampers make car hire unattractive for most visitors.

➡ London was the world's first major city to introduce a congestion charge to reduce the flow of traffic into its centre. For full details look at www. tfl.gov.uk/roadusers/congestioncharging.

➡ The following car-rental agencies have several branches across the capital: **easyCar** (www.easycar. com), **Avis** (www.avis.com), **Hertz** (www.hertz.com).

➡ Cars drive on the left in the UK.

➡ All drivers and passengers must wear seatbelts and motorcyclists must wear a helmet.

Essential Information

Business Hours

☑ **Top Tip** London is open for business every day of the year, except Christmas Day (25 December) when absolutely everything shuts down, including the transport network.

Information	9am-5pm Mon-Fri
Sights	10am-6pm
Banks	9am-5pm Mon-Fri
Shops	9am-7pm Mon-Sat, 11am-5pm Sun
Restaurants	noon-2.30pm & 6-11pm
Pubs & bars	11am-11pm

Discount Cards

➡ **London Pass** (www.londonpass.com; per 1/2/3/6 days £47/64/77/102) offers free entry and queue-jumping to major attractions; check the website for details.

➡ Passes can be tailored to include use of the Underground and buses.

Electricity

230V/50Hz

Emergency

➡ Dial ☎ 999 to call the police, fire brigade or ambulance in an emergency.

Money

☑ **Top Tip** Some large stores also take euros.

➡ The unit of currency of the UK is the pound sterling (£).

➡ One pound sterling consists of 100 pence (called 'p' colloquially).

➡ Notes come in denominations of £5, £10, £20 and £50; coins are 1p, 2p, 5p, 10p, 20p, 50p, £1 and £2.

ATMs

➡ Ubiquitous ATMs generally accept Visa, MasterCard, Cirrus or Maestro cards and more obscure ones.

➡ There is usually a transaction surcharge for cash withdrawals with foreign cards.

➡ Nonbank-run ATMs that charge £1.50 to £2 per transaction are usually found inside shops (and are particularly expensive for foreign bank card holders); look for 'Free cash withdrawals' signs to avoid these.

Changing Money

➡ The best place to change money is in any local post office branch, where no commission is charged.

➡ You can also change money in most high-street banks and some travel-agent chains, as well as at the numerous

Money-Saving Tips

➡ Visit free museums and sights.

➡ Buy an Oyster Card.

➡ Take the bus.

bureaux de change across London.

Credit & Debit Cards

➡ Credit and debit cards are accepted almost universally in London, from restaurants and bars to shops and even some taxis.

➡ American Express and Diner's Club are less widely used than Visa and MasterCard.

➡ If your card is equipped with a chip, make sure you learn the pin or you may not be permitted to pay by card.

Tipping

➡ Many restaurants add a 'discretionary' service charge to your bill; it's legal but should be clearly advertised. In places that don't, you are expected to leave a 10% to 15% tip (unless service was unsatisfactory).

➡ No need to tip to have your pint pulled or wine poured in a pub.

Public Holidays

New Year's Day 1 January

Good Friday Late March/April

Easter Monday Late March/April

Dos and Don'ts

Do

➡ Stand on the right on escalators and walk on the left.

➡ Let others off the tube before you get on.

➡ Expect traffic to stop at zebra crossings.

➡ Look right first when crossing the road.

Don't

➡ Forget your umbrella.

➡ Forget to queue for virtually everything.

➡ Forget to open doors for others.

May Day Holiday First Monday in May

Spring Bank Holiday Last Monday in May

Summer Bank Holiday Last Monday in August

Christmas Day 25 December

Boxing Day 26 December

Safe Travel

☑ **Top Tip** Pickpocketing does happen, particularly in crowded areas such as the Underground, so be discreet with your smartphone/tablet.

➡ London's a fairly safe city considering its size, so exercising common sense should keep you safe.

Telephone

➡ Some public phones still accept coins, but most take phonecards (available from retailers, including most post offices and some newsagents) or credit cards.

➡ Phone codes worth knowing:

International dialling code (☎00)

Local call rate applies (☎08457)

National call rate applies (☎0870/0871)

Premium rate applies (☎09) From 60p per minute.

Toll-free (☎0800)

Calling London

➡ London's area code is ☎020, followed by an eight-digit number.

➡ If calling London from abroad, dial your country's international access code, then 44 (the UK's country code), then 20 (ie dropping the initial 0), followed by the eight-digit phone number.

International Calls & Rates

➡ International direct dialling (IDD) calls to almost anywhere can be made from most public telephones.

➡ Many telephone calling shops and internet cafes offer cheap international calls; in such shops you phone from a metered booth.

➡ PIN-activated international calling cards, available at most corner shops, are usually the cheapest way to call abroad.

➡ Skype can be restricted in hostels and internet cafes due to noise and/or bandwidth issues.

Mobile Phones

➡ The UK uses the GSM 900 network, which covers Europe, Australia and New Zealand, but is

Visa Requirements

Country	Tourism	Work	Study
European Economic Area	x	x	x
Australia, Canada, New Zealand, South Africa, USA	x (up to 6 months)	√	√
Other nationalities	√	√	√

not compatible with the North American GSM 1900 or Japanese mobile technology.

➡ If you have a GSM phone, enquire with your service provider about roaming charges.

➡ It's usually better to buy a local SIM card from any mobile phone shop (ensure your handset is unlocked).

Tourist Information

Visit London (☎0870 156 6366; www.visitlondon.com)

City of London Information Centre (Map p92, C3; www.visitthecity.co.uk; St Paul's Churchyard, EC4; ⊙9.30am-5.30pm Mon-Sat, 10am-4pm Sun; ⊖St Paul's)

Greenwich Tourist Office (Map p166, C3; www.visitgreenwich.org.uk/tourist-

information-centre; Pepys House, 2 Cutty Sark Gardens, SE10; ⊙10am-5pm; ℝDLR Cutty Sark)

Travellers with Disabilities

➡ New hotels and modern tourist attractions are legally required to be accessible to people in wheelchairs, but many historic buildings, B&Bs and guesthouses are in older buildings, which are hard (if not impossible) to adapt.

➡ Only 66 of London's 270 tube stations have step-free access; the rest of them have escalators or stairs.

➡ The DLR is entirely accessible for wheelchair users.

→ All buses are low-floor vehicles and wheelchair users travel free.

→ Transport for London publishes the *Getting Around London* guide, which contains the latest information on accessibility for passengers with disabilities. Download it from www.tfl.gov.uk.

Visas

Immigration to the UK is becoming tougher, particularly for those seeking to work or study. Make sure you check www.uk visas.gov.uk or with your local British embassy for the most up-to-date information.

Behind the Scenes

Send Us Your Feedback

We love to hear from travellers – your comments help make our books better. We read every word, and we guarantee that your feedback goes straight to the authors. Visit **lonelyplanet.com/contact** to submit your updates and suggestions.

Note: We may edit, reproduce and incorporate your comments in Lonely Planet products such as guidebooks, websites and digital products, so let us know if you don't want your comments reproduced or your name acknowledged. For a copy of our privacy policy visit lonelyplanet.com/privacy.

Our Readers

Many thanks to the travellers who wrote to us with useful advice and anecdotes:

Bex Sheehy, Gaye Tirimanne, James Rea

Emilie's Thanks

Many thanks to fellow *London* authors Steve Fallon, Damian Harper and Vesna Maric for providing such rich pickings (and weekend inspiration!). Thanks also to all the friends who joined in the research, and to my husband, Adolfo.

Acknowledgments

Cover photograph: Tower Bridge, Maurizio Rellini/4Corners.

This Book

This 4th edition of Lonely Planet's *Pocket London* guidebook was researched and written by Emilie Filou. The 3rd edition was written by Damian Harper and the 2nd by Joe Bindloss and Sarah Johnstone. This guidebook was commissioned in Lonely Planet's London office, and produced by the following:

Commissioning Editors James Smart, Joanna Cooke **Coordinating Editors** Kirsten Rawlings, Alison Ridgway **Senior Cartographers** Jennifer Johnston, Anthony Phelan **Book Designer** Wendy Wright **Managing Editors** Martine Power, Angela Tinson **Senior Editor** Karyn Noble **Assisting Editors** Kate Morgan, Sally O'Brien **Assisting Cartographer** James Leversha **Cover Research** Naomi Parker **Thanks to** Anita Banh, Ryan Evans, Larissa Frost, Briohny Hooper, Genesys India, Jouve India, Andi Jones, Wayne Murphy, Chad Parkhill, Trent Paton, Gerard Walker

Index

See also separate subindexes for:

Eating p221
Drinking p221
Entertainment p222
Shopping p223

Sights p000
Map Pages **p000**

Sights p000
Map Pages **p000**

Our Writers

Emilie Filou

Emilie was born in Paris, where she lived until she was 18. Following her three-year degree and three gap years, she found herself in London, fell in love with the place and never really left. She now works as a journalist, specialising in Africa, and makes regular trips to the region from her home in North London. For Lonely Planet, she has contributed to guides on her native France, West Africa, Tunisia and Madagascar. She has also worked on two editions of the *London* guide and enjoyed discovering South London (almost!) as much as her home patch. You can see her work on www.emiliefilou.com; she tweets at @EmilieFilou.

Contributing Writers

Steve Fallon contributed to Westminster Abbey & Westminster, National Gallery & Covent Garden, British Museum & Bloomsbury, St Paul's & the City.

Damian Harper contributed to Kensington Museums.

Vesna Maric contributed to A Night out in Shoreditch.

Published by Lonely Planet Publications Pty Ltd
ABN 36 005 607 983
4th edition – March 2014
ISBN 978 1 74220 8763
© Lonely Planet 2014 Photographs © as indicated 2014
10 9 8 7 6 5 4 3
Printed in China